THE

POWER

OF

RETURN

The
Power
of
Return

"Return to Me That I May Return to You"

John Goyette

DESTINY IMAGE® PUBLISHERS, INC.
P.O. Box 310, Shippensburg, PA 17257-0310

"Speaking to the Purposes of God for This Generation and for the Generations to Come."

This book and all other Destiny Image, Revival Press, MercyPlace, Fresh Bread, Destiny Image Fiction, and Treasure House books are available at Christian bookstores and distributors worldwide.

For a U.S. bookstore nearest you, call **1-800-722-6774.**

For more information on foreign distributors, call **717-532-3040.**

Reach us on the Internet: **www.destinyimage.com.**

ISBN 10: 0-7684-3154-9

ISBN 13: 978-0-7684-3154-4

For Worldwide Distribution, Printed in the U.S.A.

1 2 3 4 5 6 7 8 9 10 11 / 13 12 11 10

DEDICATION

This book is dedicated to strong godly leaders—the faithful pastors of local churches and to all who hunger with them to see the Church return to the Lord and be empowered with His presence. May you *"be steadfast, immovable, always abounding in the work of the Lord, knowing that your toil is not in vain in the Lord"* (1 Cor. 15:58).

ACKNOWLEDGMENTS

I am grateful to my wife for her loving support in this project, my church, which continues to patiently encourage me in the pursuit of God's plan, and my missionary friend Professor Marvin Gilbert of Cape Theological Seminary, Bloubergrant, South Africa. His editing skills, biblical insight, and grammatical knowledge have made the message of *The Power of Return* immeasurably clear, powerful, and readable. I am also thankful for my friend and sister in the Lord, Marcia Meerwarth, who spent uncounted hours proofreading successive editions of the manuscript and never ceased to encourage me.

ENDORSEMENTS

It doesn't take long for the prospective reader to conclude that this is an ingenious book. I wish I had written it! All who read it will benefit from it.

Revival is a most difficult subject to define, trace, or evaluate. The author skillfully defines it and traces it in the crucibles of historic revivals under Old Testament leaders. The graphs of comparisons early in the book arouse the reader's interests in revivals and allow us all to study these awakenings objectively; all who read it will have a chance to observe and evaluate movements and be a part of sustaining them until revivals result.

The book contains stunning insights, reasonable evaluations, and practical guidance. It is thoroughly biblical, solidly practical, and personally challenging. It throbs with life and light.

Thanks, John, for this astounding contribution.

Jack Taylor
President of Dimensions Ministries
Melbourne, Florida

WOW! Great stuff! I read it and was genuinely refreshed in spirit and challenged. It was thoroughly solid theologically. I have felt, myself, for a long time that revival is not a "happenstance" thing—that there are "principles" that bring revival. You have a very healthy and biblical approach to the subject, very refreshing. I really think some of the revivals that have gotten started didn't flash into full flame because they were missing some of the critical points you make in *The Power of Return*.

Dennis Marquardt
District Superintendent of the Northern New England District of the Assemblies of God

"Return to Me" declares the Lord of hosts, *"that I may return to you"* (Zechariah 1:3).

CONTENTS

PREFACE

In the following pages you will read about 12 great revivals recorded in the Bible. For the most part, they are unfamiliar to contemporary Christians, even though large sections of Scripture are devoted to each account and many of the prophetic books relate to these awakenings. Several of the heroes and heroines in these revivals are almost completely unknown to the Church. In a time when we hear a great deal concerning revival, it is strange that the greatest resource in existence about spiritual awakenings, Scripture itself, is largely ignored.

Ignorance of these revivals can be partially attributed to the fact that the words *revive, revived, renewal, renew,* and *renewed* are used sparingly in the Bible. None of these words is found in Second Chronicles, the Bible book with the most revival accounts. Stunningly, the word *revival* does not appear in the entire NASB, KJV, or NIV Bible. God simply uses different terminology to speak of what we call revival. Therefore, the typical method of study for a person interested in the subject of revival—using a concordance—does not bring the individual to these accounts. As a result, these revivals have not received the attention and study they deserve.

The revival accounts in this book are not chosen arbitrarily. All the scriptural accounts of revival significant in length and detail are included. A case could be made for including the Exodus from Egypt as a revival, since the Israelites were already covenant people of God. But the Exodus is more properly seen as an analogy of conversion rather than revival. While the Book of Judges also tracks cycles of spiritual decline and revival, most are relatively limited in scope and detail. Champions of God arose including Samson, Gideon, and Jepthah, but except for the time under Samuel's leadership, prolonged revival did not take place. Jonah is usually considered a revival book, but I don't include it in my list, as it is not really the account of a revival but of an evangelistic outreach to an unsaved population. The focus of the Book of Jonah is actually on a reluctant evangelist and his spiritual problem. The city of Nineveh temporarily turned to God, but this was not a renewal of God's people.

It is my fervent prayer that a fresh look at the 12 great revival accounts God recorded and preserved for us might give us wisdom and encouragement to prepare a spiritual atmosphere ready to ignite at the flame of God's presence.

Chapter 1

SETTING THE STAGE FOR REVIVAL

I can still vividly recall the expanding ball of flames enveloping me. Stunned by the searing blaze fueled by gasoline fumes, I checked to see if I was still in one piece—though my clothing bore burn marks, and much of my hair, eyebrows, and mustache were turned to ashes by the fireball, I was unhurt. I staggered to the other end of the large brush pile to find my friend Paul lying on the ground, similarly singed. Surrounded by the stench of burnt hair, we knelt in the wet grass and gave thanks to God we were still alive.

The night had started wonderfully. Paul and his wife, Deb, friends of ours from church, had invited a few couples to share a meal at their house; the evening was to conclude with a bonfire. Following dinner, Paul, I, and a couple of the other men went out to the field behind their house where a large brush pile waited to be burned. The evening air was dead still, cool, and wet. A light rain had been falling for some time. To give the fire a good start in the wet conditions, we poured gasoline in strategic spots around the 40-foot-wide mound and placed wadded-up newspapers at either end of the pile. Unseen, gas fumes gathered under the drooping canopy of limbs still carrying their leaves, forming an explosive fuel-air mixture. Paul handed me one of two small propane-fueled lighters. Taking the other, he went to the far end of the mound. Simultaneously, we struck the ignition triggers. The fumes exploded, producing a powerful "whump" that shook the house 75 yards away and ignited the ball of flames that had encompassed us.

Unwittingly, my friend and I had set the stage for this memorable experience. The spark from the lighters had ignited the charged atmosphere that had developed at the brush pile. In the same way, if the right conditions in the spiritual realm exist among believers, the spark of God's presence will kindle revival in the Church.

Some local churches are experiencing God's fiery presence. On the whole, however, we cannot deny the need for the illuminating, cleansing warmth of heavenly fire in the Church today. Despite God's loving faithfulness, the sad, consistent testimony of both Scripture and church history is that *God's people fall into a lukewarm state—even apostasy—with alarming regularity.* Christians need times of radical recommitment and refreshing. We have a tendency to establish religious traditions that must be challenged and sometimes dismantled. We can harbor pharisaical, prideful attitudes, and many are bound by ungodly strongholds of habit. Worldliness in the form of greed, bitterness, rebellion, and sexual sin are common in the Lord's house. Who can deny the obvious need for revival?

The flames passing over my friend and me that night made some changes in us—we now have a deeper respect for the combination of fire and gasoline. Beside this new-found wisdom, our appearance was modified. Similarly, heavenly fire passing over our churches will transform God's people. Actually, the changes will be much deeper and more permanent; for the flames of revival bring wisdom and profound alterations in attitude and behavior.

The blessings of spiritual renewal are much to be desired. Scriptural and historical accounts offer proof that times of revival bring change to the Church, evidenced by heightened spiritual life and power. When revival fire falls, the Word of God is preached with powerful anointing. Love becomes the watchword. The power and gifts of the Holy Spirit flow like a river, and supernatural healings regularly confirm the Word. Repentance wells up in hearts exposed to the life-giving message of the Gospel and many are converted. When spiritual opposition assails the revived church, it is met with divine intervention, just as God stayed the moon in the Valley of Aijalon for Joshua (see Josh. 10:12), and struck down attacking armies as He did for Asa and Jehoshaphat.

Most Christians do not doubt the need for revival; nor do we question God's promise to renew His people. The question is, how can a needy church enter into that promise? Therein lies a difficulty—many of those in the pulpit have been taught or have come to believe that revival is totally beyond our control. Consequently, most in the pew believe this also. Most view revival as exclusively God's choice. In other words, the Church believes that the Lord pours out times of refreshing in what seems to be a rather haphazard manner without much regard to what is happening in the local church or region. If this is true, it means we can only hope and pray that revival will come our way.

While God is sovereign and certainly acts as He chooses, the thought that God behaves capriciously or with partiality is inconsistent with what we know of His nature and desire. He wants to revive lukewarm, dying, and worldly churches more than these churches desire his reviving fire. God is neither capricious nor inconsistent. He is a God of purpose and plan. He simply waits for His conditions to be met; when they are, He manifests His presence in undeniable power and blessing—what we call revival.

We cannot engineer what the Lord will do; yet, relegating ourselves to pleading and waiting for a move of God is not the sole option. The situation at the brush pile that night illustrates this point. The fireball was unplanned. It was the result of a chance combination of circumstances:

the still night, the leaves on the branches, and our unwise decision to use gasoline to prime the fire. It was an accident. Sometimes we have accidental revival in church. *The right elements come together by chance and there is a spiritual explosion.*

The premise of this book is that instead of simply hoping and praying that God will sprinkle revival in our area or that accidental revival will develop in our churches, we can proactively prepare an explosive spiritual atmosphere, ready to be ignited by the spark of God's presence. When a favorable environment exists, the Lord willingly kindles a flame. A study of the great revivals recorded in God's Word confirms that the Lord's people have a necessary part to play in ushering in times of awakening.

Intentionally pursuing revival is not questioning the sovereignty of God, as some say. It is cooperating with His desire to partner with humankind. I began to recognize this principle some years ago when studying the dedication of Solomon's Temple. Questions gripped me as I read Second Chronicles 7:1, *"Fire came down from heaven and consumed the burnt offering and the sacrifices, and the glory of the Lord filled the house."* Why did fire fall and glory fill the house? Why did God appear in such a powerful way that day? Was this response due to the perfection of Solomon's prayer? Was it because of the beauty of the building? Solomon prayed admirably, and the Temple was indeed a special building. Even so, I realized as I poured over the preceding chapters that the fire fell that day because Solomon and the people followed a Spirit-led plan that had started years earlier. This could be described as God's people partnering or cooperating with Him by doing what they were supposed to do. As they did so, a situation developed so favorable to the Lord revealing His manifest presence that God did not hold back His glory and fire.

I began finding other scriptural accounts of revival and studied them to see if the basic pattern found in Solomon's revival was evident. I discovered that each of the 12 major revivals in the Old Testament began as

God's people cooperated with him by following the same general blue-print. This blueprint—what I call the revival protocol—gives us guidance for returning to the Lord. This process of returning to God sets the stage for His presence to be made manifest in our midst. "'Return to Me,' declares the Lord of hosts, 'that I may return to you'" (Zech. 1:3). Before examining the revival protocol in detail, it will be helpful to define the terms:

Revival: *Biblical revival is actually a two-stage process.* The first stage of revival is a return of God's people to Him.[1] This requires a fundamental realignment of believers' affection for God and obedience to Him, result-ing in a positive change in attitudes and actions.

The second stage of revival is a gracious response by the Lord to His returning people. This is often seen as the "revival." It is characterized by supernatural displays of His presence and/or protection, miraculous encouragement, and copious amounts of grace—all leading to greater unity, worship, and joy. Widespread repentance and conversion among the lost accompany this stage.

Protocol: World leaders and nations recognize protocol whenever dealing with dignitaries, foreign diplomats, and heads of state. Protocol expresses *etiquette* that displays appropriate honor for individuals, their rela-tionships, and any agreements they have reached. Protocol determines the *proper conduct* in these situations. The word *protocol* is also used to describe *standard procedures* for the medical, scientific, and computer fields.

Revival protocol then, *is the etiquette and proper conduct expected by our heavenly Head of State. It is the standard procedure to use when returning to Him.*

Revival protocol consists of 20 elements repeatedly evident in the accounts of major revivals in the Bible. Taken together, they define the etiquette, conduct, and procedure for returning to the Lord and inviting His presence. A consistent, albeit not identical, pattern using these com-ponents can be traced in each of the 12 major Old Testament revivals.

The first five components are nonnegotiable. They are present in each of the 12 revivals. All 20 components are important, and each revival has more than these core five. Even so, they are apparently essential in returning to God:

1. Strong godly leader

2. Shared vision

3. Return to the Word

4. Gathering in unity

5. Obedience to authority

6. Praise/worship

7. United prayer

8. Giving/tithing

9. Covenant

10. Offerings of sacrifice

11. Concern for the temple

12. Confession/repentance

13. Consecration

14. Destruction of idols

15. Prophetic ministry

16. Construction project

17. Fasting

18. Gathering of leaders

19. Teaching ministry

20. Moving forward

Table 1, on pages 24 and 25, shows the components that were present in each of the 12 revivals discussed in this book.

It is encouraging to note that perfection in following the protocol is not necessary for God to respond. Thankfully, we don't have to be faultless to succeed in cooperating with God. Every strong godly leader in Scripture had a heart aflame for God but also had feet of clay: David struggled with lust; Solomon set up idols for his foreign wives; Joash showed weak character; Hezekiah became prideful. In addition, the people sometimes failed to follow through wholeheartedly. They intermarried with other nations and satanic high places were repeatedly rebuilt. The revival protocol was never applied perfectly in the 12 scriptural examples. However, when it was implemented, even imperfectly, it always led to a gracious response from the Lord.

Just as we can chart the components of a return to the Lord, we can chart the results of that return—stage two revival (See Table 2 on pages 26 and 27). The return of the Lord's manifest presence and intervention in stage-two revival brought blessings to God's people and increased their desire to please Him. Fifteen distinct spiritual results can be identified:

1. Miracles/victory

2. Praise/worship

3. Great joy

4. Others come in

5. Peace

6. Ministry set in order

7. Sacrifices offered

8. Giving/tithing

9. Inheritance restored

10. Passover observed

11. Separation from world

12. Idols destroyed

13. Covenant made

TABLE 1 COMPARISON OF COMPONENTS OF THE REVIVAL PROTOCOL APPLIED IN THE MAJOR OLD TESTAMENT REVIVALS

Components	Stage One Revivals			
1. Strong Godly Leader	Joshua	Samuel	David	Solomon
2. Shared Vision	Enter the land	The people return to God	Bring the Ark into the city	Build the Temple
3. The Word of God	X	X	X	X
4. Gathering in Unity	X	X	X	X
5. Obedience to Authority	X	X	X	X
6. Praise/Worship	X	X	X	X
7. United Prayer		X		X
8. Giving/Tithing	X		X	X
9. Covenant	X			X
10. Sacrifices		X	X	X
11. Concern for the Temple			X	X
12. Confession/Repentance	X	X		X
13. Consecration	X	X		X
14. Destruction of Idols		X		
15. Prophetic Ministry		X	X	
16. Building Project				X
17. Fasting		X	X	
18. Gathering of Leaders			X	X
19. Teaching Ministry				
20. Forward Movement	X			
Major Lessons	Gilgal	Prayer power	Do it God's way	Obedience
Problem Areas	Overconfidence	Disobedient sons	Ignorance of Scripture	Built idols

TABLE 1 CONTINUED

Stage One Revivals						
Asa	Jehoshaphat	Hezekiah	Joash	Josiah	Zerubbabel	Ezra
All seek God	Cleanse the land of idols	Consecrate temple & workers	Crown the true king	Repair God's House	Rebuild the Temple	Know, teach, live the Word
X	X	X	X	X	X	X
X	X	X	X	X	X	X
X	X	X	X	X	X	X
	X	X	X	X	X	X
X	X	X			X	X
X			X	X	X	
X		X	X	X		
		X		X	X	
		X		X	X	X
				X		X
		X		X		
X	X	X		X		
	X	X		X	X	
X		X			X	
	X					X
		X	X			
X	X					X
					X	X
Depend on God	Praise power	Consecration	Power of influence	Find the Book	Prophet power	Confess Repent
Jailed a prophet	Hearts not wholly given	Pride	Weak character	Alliance with Ahab	Discouragement	Intermarriage

TABLE 2 RESULTS OF APPLYING THE REVIVAL PROTOCOL

Results	Stage Two Revivals				
	Joshua	Samuel	David	Solomon	Asa
1. Opposition	X	X	X	X	X
2. Miracle or Victory	X	X	X	X	X
3. Praise/Worship		X	X	X	X
4. Great joy	X	X	X	X	X
5. More people/converts			X	X	X
6. Peace	X	X	X	X	X
7. Ministry set in order			X	X	
8. Sacrifices offered			X	X	X
9. Giving/Tithing					X
10. Restoration of inheritance		X			X
11. Passover	X				
12. Separation from the world					
13. Destruction of idols					X
14. Covenant					X

14. Healing

15. Opposition

Generally speaking, the greatest effectiveness of the protocol was obtained when the largest number of components was put in place over the longest period of time. In brief, the more components present, the greater the results.

TABLE 2 CONTINUED

Stage Two Revivals						
Jehoshaphat	Hezekiah	Joash	Josiah	Zerubbabel	Ezra	Nehemiah
X	X	X	X	X	X	X
X	X	X			X	X
X	X	X	X	X	X	X
X	X	X		X		X
X	X	X	X	X	X	
X	X	X				X
	X	X	X	X		X
	X			X		
	X	X	X			X
				X	X	X
	X		X			
				X	X	X
	X					
		X				

Some of the results in stage two revivals, such as praise/worship, giving/tithing, offerings of sacrifice, the destruction of idols, and making of covenant also appear as components in the initial effort to return to God. The difference is that in stage two revivals these results were done in acknowledgement and appreciation of the Lord's presence and power rather than in preparation.

Opposition is a result that is present in all of the biblical revivals.[2] We must expect, and be prepared to struggle with, the kingdom of darkness when we return to God. Scripture and experience teach us that criticism will pursue even the greatest revivals. God's enemies will angrily oppose any move to restore power and life to the Church. Others, who do not fully understand the ways of God, will object to things that happen when human beings are in the white-hot fire of revival. Valid objections can arise as well; for, revival leaders and their followers make mistakes, as is evidenced in the accounts we will examine. However, when spiritual renewal is based on the scriptural principles of the revival protocol, the genuine nature of what occurs will speak for itself. A church filled with Christians walking in holiness, loving God and people, living transformed lives, not to mention the display of supernatural power and conversion of lost souls will validate the reality of revival.

Concerns about what happens in revival beg the question, "What should revival look like?" While it is easy to say, "We just want what God wants," having a clear picture of what revival really entails will help us immeasurably as we pursue a move of God. Vision is critically important—*"Where there is no vision, the people perish"* (Prov. 29:18). Here again, a knowledge of the scriptural awakenings can help us. Each leader of the 12 major revivals had a powerful vision he vigorously pursued.

1. Joshua was determined to lead Israel into the Promised Land (see Josh. 1,3-6).

2. Samuel longed to see the people return to God and conquer the Philistines (see 1 Sam. 7).

3. David wanted to bring the Ark of the Covenant to Jerusalem (see 1 Chron. 13,15-16; 2 Sam. 5-6).

4. Solomon obediently received the vision of building the Temple from his father and made it his own (see 2 Chron. 28–2 Chron. 7; 1 Kings 6-8).

5. Asa discovered the power of prayer and wanted all Judah to seek the Lord (see 2 Chron. 14-16; 1 Kings 15:8-24).

6. Jehoshaphat was set on cleansing the land of idols (see 2 Chron. 17-20).

7. Hezekiah commanded the priests and Levites to consecrate themselves and the Temple to God (see 2 Chron. 29-31; 2 Kings 18-19).

8. Jehoiada was determined to depose the evil authority of Athaliah and crown the true King (see 2 Chron. 23-24; 2 Kings 11-12).

9. Josiah's vision was that the people would agree to "perform the words of the covenant written in the book" (2 Chron. 34:31-32).

10. Zerubbabel's vision was to rebuild the Temple that had been destroyed (see Ezra 1-6).

11. Ezra set his heart to know, teach, and live the Word of God in Israel (see Ezra 7-10).

12. Nehemiah had a deep burden to rebuild the city wall of Jerusalem (see Neh. 1-13).

When taken together in the light of the New Testament, these individual visions give us a description of what should happen in a present-day revival. They lead us to see revival as a time when the Church enters into the promise of a victorious life (the Joshua vision); Christians experience triumph over the flesh (the Samuel vision); the presence of the Lord is carried into our services by consecrated servants of God (the David vision); the Church is built up in beauty and is a house of prayer (the Solomon and Asa visions); false gods are removed from our hearts as we seek the Lord (the Jehoshaphat and Hezekiah visions); ungodly authority supplanting the place of Jesus in the Church is removed (the Joash/Jehoiada vision); the Bible is rediscovered among God's people (the Josiah vision); the Church is set free from captivity caused by apostasy, and worship is restored (the Zerubbabel vision); God's people set their hearts to know, teach, and live the Word of God (the Ezra vision), and Christian character is rebuilt in our lives, homes, and churches (the Nehemiah vision). It is important to understand that these individual revival visions are all elements of stage one revival—the return of the Church to God. The other things we crave—the manifest presence of God, various miracles, raising the dead, healing the sick, and the conversion of large numbers of unbelievers—are all elements of stage two revivals.

Recognizing the value of the revival protocol does not minimize the centrality of Jesus Christ and the influence of the Holy Spirit in the life of the Church. All revivals must be led by the Spirit of God and focus on God's Son. Obviously, there can be no revival without Jesus. He is the center of all Scripture. Types of Him can be found in each of the revival accounts. He is the strong and godly leader. He is the magnanimous King and the obedient Son. He is the Word. He is the suckling Lamb offered up by Samuel. He is the house of the Lord. The list goes on and on. In addition, the Holy Spirit is faithful to convict us of our need to return to the Lord and lead us in applying the elements of the revival protocol. After all, a plan found in Scripture must, of necessity, have been birthed by the Holy Spirit.

GOD'S GOT A PLAN!

Knowing that a God-given plan leading to revival exists frees us from unproductive syndromes that can cause frustration. The first one of these frustrating syndromes we might call *running after revival*. This occurs when believers try to "get revival" by traveling far and wide to churches experiencing a move of God. I don't want to discourage people from visiting these places, for great benefits can be gained by being in such a setting. Our primary passion, however, should be preparing ourselves and our context for His supernatural presence, which will surely come as we wholeheartedly apply the principles of the revival protocol.

The second unproductive syndrome is *special speaker scheduling*. This is when we invite speaker after speaker, hoping they will bring a revival with them. Although an anointed individual can trigger a revival, the preparatory work of applying protocol principles must be done.

Understanding the revival protocol also helps us cope with the third frustration-producing syndrome—*incomplete implementation*. This may happen if we diligently practice some protocol components, and still find that revival does not blossom. For example, a church may major in a few of the 20 components, based on the scriptural record. However, if at least the five core components are not in place, there will be no heavenly fire. [3]

GOD ILLUSTRATED HIS PLAN FOR US

Some may object to using Old Testament passages to illustrate a plan for us today, but this is exactly what Romans 15:4 instructs us to do: *"Whatever was written in earlier times was written for our instruction, so that through perseverance and the encouragement of the Scriptures we might have hope."* The revival protocol does not propose a return to the Old Covenant. Rather, the protocol simply invites us to apply the timeless principles of the Kingdom.

This is not a choice of Old Testament or New Testament, for *"all Scripture is inspired by God and profitable for teaching, for reproof, for correction, for training in righteousness"* (2 Tim. 3:16). The components of the revival protocol are New Testament truths illustrated in the pages of the Old Testament. The experiences of God's people in times past reveal mistakes we can avoid and effective behavior we can emulate. In First Corinthians 10:11 Paul refers to the events in Israel's history this way: *"These things happened to them as an example, and they were written for our instruction, upon whom the ends of the ages have come."* Ignoring the scriptural record of how times of spiritual refreshing came in earlier days only hinders us in pursuing new outpourings of God's grace.

THE ONLY BIBLICAL ACCOUNTS OF REVIVAL

The Old Testament accounts of revival are especially important in light of how God structured the Bible. The Old Testament spans a time period of some 1,400 years. Consequently, we clearly see cycles of falling away and returning to God (e.g., the Book of Judges alone records several such cycles). The New Testament, on the other hand, covers a span of only 60 years (or less) of church history. As a result, the cycle of falling away from God and returning to Him is discussed, but not chronicled. Church history in the last 2,000 years, however, bears abundant witness that the cycles seen in the Old Testament continue in the Church today. Gleaning wisdom from the revival accounts that God gave us in the history of Israel is essential to encouraging and maintaining a revived state in the Church.

Scripture shows us a clear pattern to follow when returning to the Lord, but because spiritual life is about the heart and a relationship with God, we must not view the revival protocol as a *vending-machine* theology: Put in the coins of prayer, vision, unity, etc., and out pops the revival *candy bar*. Nonetheless, let us be intentional in preparing for the presence of the Lord. We must pray and hope for revival, but, in addition, let us do everything Scripture reveals to be effective in returning to the Lord, and thus set the stage for Him to do something wonderful among us.

We will examine how the components of the revival protocol were applied in the scriptural examples of revival. A dramatic narrative based on Scripture introduces each chapter bringing the revival to life, showing us that each move of God happened among real, imperfect, yet spiritually hungry people. The accounts of these revivals cause us to wonder at the displays of God's power and rejoice at the results that followed a return to God.

ENDNOTES

1. While personal revival is necessary, and the revival protocol can be applied individually, this book is primarily concerned with a pattern of *corporate* revival found in Scripture.

2. Chapter 13 deals with opposition and the correct response to it in some detail.

3. Strong godly leader, Shared vision, Return to the Word, Gathering in unity, Obedience to authority.

POINTS TO PONDER

1. Many have argued that the time and place of revivals is totally dependent on God. The idea of a "revival protocol" in which the Church has a critical part to play, flies in the face of such teaching. How do you see it?

2. Stage one revival is a return to God by His people. This return can be described as a combination of up to 20 components (see Table 1). Which 11 components are present in over half of the awakenings?

3. The author mentions that sometimes there is "accidental revival." What is meant by that, and how does it relate to the idea of intentionally preparing an atmosphere that is ready for a divine spark?

4. When God returned to His people in power there are many wonderful results (see Table 2). Which blessings occur in more than half of the revivals? Which result appeared every time God's people returned to Him?

5. What light do the great awakenings recorded in the Old Testament shed on what we should envision and desire in modern-day revivals?

Chapter 2

THE JOSHUA REVIVAL
FROM WILDERNESS TO PROMISED LAND

JOSHUA AT THE BATTLE OF JERICHO[1]

Eleazar slid his hand along the smooth gold sheathing of the pole on his shoulder. He was one of 12 men who moved in unison. They carried the Glory of Israel—the Ark of the Covenant. Eleazar rejoiced in the privilege, knowing the wings of cherubim were over his head. He was always amazed at how the weight of the solid gold angels and gold-clad chest seemed almost more than he could bear when he first lifted it. *Then Spirit-born strength would flood in, thrilling his senses and empowering him for his sacred task.* Surely, the Lord Himself helped the Levites carry the Ark.

The sun, beginning to peek over the horizon, behind him, softly illuminated the walled city that lay to his right. Eleazar scanned the entire plain ahead. As the lead priest on the right pole, he had an excellent view of the long human procession curving far ahead of him around the city. Several hundred thousand armed men stretched in a wide flow in what was now a well-worn path, circumscribing the Canaanite fortress of Jericho. They knew the path well. They had walked it once a day for six days. Behind Eleazar and his fellow priests strode a rear guard of 30,000. The women and children remained at camp.

This day would differ greatly from the previous six. The preceding days had been preparatory; today would bring triumph. The Israelites had risen well before sunrise. The camp at Gilgal had been a beehive of activity. Eleazar licked his lips. He could still taste breakfast; the wheat bread was quite different from the usual fare of crunchy sweet manna cakes. He missed those cakes, having eaten them since childhood. He had savored the grapes however, the cool tangy juice flooding his taste buds.

Eleazar, now 48, was only 10 years old the last time he tasted a grape. He recalled it was the same day the 12 men returned from scouting the territory ahead. The men had brought back a huge cluster of grapes from the Promised Land. Eleazar had been one of the fortunate ones who had tasted. Ten had proclaimed that conquering the land would be an impossible task. Fear spread like wildfire through the camp as these ten leaders of Israel described the Canaanite inhabitants, some of whom stood over nine feet tall. "We were like grasshoppers before them!" said the Ten. In sharp contrast, Joshua and Caleb argued valiantly that victory could be won with God's help. Sadly, these two brave men were shouted down by the frustrated, fearful crowd. The children of Israel, thus, lost their chance to enter the Promised Land. The sight of Moses, angry and heartbroken, was etched in Eleazar's memory. Israel—so close to the Promised Land—had simply struck their tents and headed back into the vast wilderness.

Now, on Jericho's plain, seven priests walked ahead of Eleazar and the others. The priests were blowing large rams' horns that seemed to carve the warm air, making a way for the Ark. Other priests willingly cycled in to keep the shofars sounding continuously. Eleazar's eyes found Joshua, Caleb at his side, their gray hair ruffled by the breeze. They strode confidently ahead of the trumpets. Joshua, the undisputed leader of Israel, carried a javelin as a staff.

The plan God had given to Joshua to take the city seemed outrageous; even so, Eleazar believed it would work. After all, when they crossed the Jordan in flood tide, hadn't the river meekly slowed and then stopped altogether as he and the other priests stepped into the water? God would bring the stronghold of Jericho down, and He would use Israel to do it!

Excitement and anticipation coursed through the huge mass of men like waves flowing over shoals of fear. Today was the day Jericho would fall; those imposing walls would be breached and the city would be conquered! "We must have victory," Eleazar mused. His jaw tightened as he remembered how they had buried his father and the others in dry desert ground when they fell over the long years. He lifted his eyes to the skies as he whispered to himself, *"I, for one, am not going back to wander and die in the wilderness.* God has given us this land!"

The men walked on into the morning. An hour passed and Eleazar and the other 11 surrendered their positions at the poles. The hourly shifts were taxing. Even with the Lord's help, the Ark weighed heavily on their shoulders. The thick line of marchers eventually made a complete circle around the city. By noon, the Israelites had circled the city almost three times. They kept a distance from the walls, staying well out of bow range. They could see people on the walls occasionally making gestures and mouthing faintly heard jeers and insults. Other than the shofars sounding in harmony, the huge mass of Israelites marched on in eerie silence. Eleazar's turn under the golden wings came again. With barely a pause, as his team of 12 resumed their labor, the Ark continued to move forward.

No one attempted to enter or leave the city. Jericho was large, obviously well-supplied and heavily armed. The high stone wall surrounding the city was wide enough in places to support entire houses. It offered no obvious weakness. Eleazar wondered how the wall was going to come down. He saw concern mirrored on the faces of his brethren, but no one grumbled. On they trudged around the city, four times, five. Shadows lengthened. Well into the afternoon they completed the sixth circuit of Jericho. Finally, they were on the seventh time around. Their pace had been measured and stately throughout the day, but now began to pick up speed. Grass had been worn into dust that rose in puffs under their feet. Their eyes often shifted to the grove of palm trees that was the landmark for their circular progress. Still, no one talked; Joshua had commanded silence. The leading edge of the army of men passed the palms. Eleazar could feel triumphant emotion growing in the ranks as they achieved the seventh circuit. In only minutes the Ark itself would pass the trees. Soon the plan, whatever it was, would unfold. "God will do whatever He has purposed," the priest thought to himself, "Surely the Lord God will triumph!"

Joshua stepped out of line as he reached the palms. He turned to watch the shofars pass, studying the Ark as it approached. Eleazar straightened as he felt Joshua's gaze fall on him. The Ark was well past him now, but the procession continued so that the rear guard could complete the last lap. As they did so, the huge procession slowed to a halt. The shofars that had been blown continuously since dawn, suddenly fell silent. Joshua pivoted toward the city, as did the rest, with an audible shuffle of over a million feet. Joshua waited, face lifted toward Heaven. Eleazar saw people filling the ramparts of the city wall, drawn by the silencing of the horns and the now stationary encircling throng.

All eyes were on the distinguished figure with the javelin. Slowly, he turned to point at the seven priests with the rams' horns. They put them to their lips again and blew a thunderous sustained blast that could be heard across the plain. As those clear, piercing notes faded, Joshua thrust his javelin into the air with both hands raised. Rising to his full height, he commanded in a voice that seemed to carry supernaturally, "*Shout!* For the Lord has given you the city!" Eleazar and the others were ready. As Joshua had instructed, *they took a deep breath and more than 600,000 men of Israel shouted with all their might* (see Num. 26:51). They had been quiet for seven days. Now they shouted with a great shout! *The sound welled up in a deafening wave pummeling the air.* Ebbing, then strengthening again and again, this shout of faith, obedience, and approaching victory was a palpable force.

At first, nothing seemed to happen, but as the surging waves of sound crescendoed to a climax, Eleazar saw people on the wall begin to run. The actual collapse began near the gate. Huge stones began to tremble. In one grinding motion around the city, mortar suddenly lost its bond. In a crashing, crushing jumble of rocks, the wall fell. The rumble of the collapse began to give way to the sound of screams coming from within the city.

Eleazar noticed that a curiously small portion of the wall, with a house perched stubbornly on top, still stood. While Eleazar and his cohorts remained with the Ark and the rear guard, the army of wilderness-hardened men advanced on the remnants of a city now shrouded by a huge, billowing cloud of dust.

THE SETTING FOR REVIVAL

Some might wonder if the story of Israel crossing the Jordan River, the battle of Jericho, and the subsequent settlement of the Promised Land ought to be included in the revival protocol, but this certainly was a revival situation. In many ways, it is the prototypical revival. The children of Israel came out of Egypt and arrived at the entrance to the Promised Land two years later. Because of rebellion motivated by a lack of faith, they refused to enter the land. As a result, they spent the next 38 years in the wilderness. Except for those first two years, *the wilderness experience was a lengthy, needless detour filled with pain, regret, and longing for what could have been.* The generation of Israelites preparing to enter Canaan under Joshua's leadership had never shared a Passover. They were not circumcised, nor were they living in, and, enjoying their inheritance.

Their story is an analogy of the Christian experience. The Israelites were liberated from Egypt and Pharaoh's dominion. This represents our deliverance from the world and freedom from satan. The initial two years in the wilderness was a time of revelation and training. The subsequent decades of wilderness wanderings illustrate the experience of Christians who are in covenant relationship with God, yet because of fear and some degree of rebellion, fail to enter a victorious Christian life.

After the death of that rebellious and fearful Israelite generation, God brought their descendants back to the edge of Canaan. This illustrates the mercy and love of God, for the Promised Land represents the abundant and victorious Christian life we are privileged to enter (or return to, if we need to be revived).

STAGE ONE REVIVAL (GOD'S PEOPLE RETURN TO HIM)

The scriptural accounts of revival always include a key leader. These leaders were catalysts for change. Joshua was one of the best of these **strong godly leaders** (revival protocol component #1).[2] For 40 years Joshua was privileged to be the protégé of one of the greatest men of all time. Together with Moses, Joshua saw the Lord on Mount Sinai (see Exod. 24:13) and heard God's voice in the tent of meeting (see Exod. 33:11). He demonstrated courage and skill on the battlefield against the

Amalekites (see Exod. 17:13) and was a man of proven character. Now it would be Joshua, not Moses, who would take the children of Israel into the Promised Land. Moses was 120 years old, and a new leader was needed. In addition, Moses could not enter the Promised Land because of the incident at Meribah, where he angrily struck the rock instead of speaking to it, as the Lord had commanded (see Num. 20:11).

There was another reason Moses could not lead Israel into the Promised Land. Moses, as the lawgiver, represents the Law. Even the most diligent adherence to the Law will never lead us into the abundant Christian life. Entrance into all that God has promised us must be by grace through faith. Joshua's name (*Y'shua* in Hebrew) means "the Lord is salvation." We spell this name today J-E-S-U-S. His very name represents grace. Jesus, not Moses, is the one who leads us into our promised inheritance.

By faith, the children of Israel **shared a vision** (Component #2) of leaving the wilderness and possessing the Promised Land. We also need to look forward by faith to see the vision of revival, of living in obedience, righteousness, and victory. The land of Canaan is beautifully and clearly described in terms that will help us cultivate a desire for the spiritual Promised Land:

First, the land was a gift. God told Joshua; *"Every place on which the sole of your foot treads, I have given it to you"* (Josh. 1:3). Notice that although the land was given, it still had to be conquered. They had to "tread upon" it. *Similarly, our title to the victorious life is the gift of God, but possession demands an obedient walk.*

Second, God also revealed to Joshua that the land was large; *"From the wilderness and this Lebanon, even as far as the great river, the river Euphrates, all the land of the Hittites, and as far as the Great Sea toward the setting of the sun will be your territory"* (Josh. 1:4). The spiritual Promised Land of revival is expansive.

Third, Deuteronomy 8:7-9 relates that the Lord God was bringing Israel into a pleasant and productive place:

> [It is] *a good land, a land of brooks of water, of fountains and springs, flowing forth in valleys and hills; a land of wheat and barley, of vines and fig trees and pomegranates, a land of olive oil and honey.*

God assured them that Canaan would be a place of plenty and thanksgiving:

> [It is] *a land where you will eat food without scarcity, in which you will not lack anything; a land whose stones are iron, and out of whose hills you can dig copper. When you have eaten and are satisfied, you shall bless the Lord your God for the good land which He has given you* (Deuteronomy 8:9-10).

Fourth, the Promised Land would also be a place of victory. The Lord said to Joshua, *No man shall be able to stand against you all the days of your life, as I was with Moses so I will be with you* (see Josh. 1:5). In other words, when you enter the land, you are going to have to fight, but with God's help, you will win. Though conflict would abound in the Promised Land, victory was assured. These qualities of the Promised Land illustrate to us that the abundant life is available to us as a gift. It is an extensive and wonderful *land* in which we find all we need in every area of our lives. And while strongholds must be torn down and *giants* must be slain, we know that Jesus is with us in the struggle and the power of God is undergirding us.

The wilderness was supposed to be a temporary experience for the Israelites. Instead, it became a life-long dwelling place for a generation of them. Similarly, *the church may experience a transitional time of wilderness travel to promised blessing but spiritual wilderness is not to be the norm.* Realizing the stark contrast between the wilderness and the Promised Land will help us be determined to abandon the status quo and press forward into revival. Reasons abound for choosing to leave the wilderness and endeavoring to cross the spiritual Jordan:

First, the wilderness was a place of bare survival, of minimal existence. Israel had manna every morning and shoes that never wore out. It was life with God, but it was still a life of frustration. The promised inheritance remained a mystery. Israel did not even enjoy a glimpse of the land filled with milk and honey. Christians *can* survive in the wilderness, but they *do not* experience all that God has promised.

Second, the wilderness was a place of restlessness and insecurity. Israel never knew from one day to the next where they would lay their heads. They wandered about without destination, simply marking time until death overtook them. The wilderness life for a Christian is one of restless insecurity in body, mind, and spirit.

Third, the wilderness was a place of discontent. Murmuring and complaining against God and His chosen leadership was endemic among the people (see Num. 11,12,14,16). What God provided was never enough, nor good enough for that generation. Similarly, Christians living in the spiritual desert are preoccupied with troubles and dissatisfaction and are often found murmuring against God and their leaders.

Fourth, the wilderness was fruitless; it was dry and barren. Israel did not plant nor harvest for 40 years. Similarly, fruitful productive Christians are rarely found in the spiritual wilderness.

Fifth, many in the wilderness wavered in their commitment. It was a place of vacillation. The Israelites could not decide if they really wanted to enter the Promised Land. Moses led Israel out of Egypt; the lingering challenge Moses faced was getting *Egypt out of the Israelites.* Their experience in the desert was like a roller coaster ride. As long as things went well, they followed Moses willingly. When life became difficult, however, they wanted to return to Egypt—this in spite of the fact that Egypt enslaved them and murdered their children. Those living in the wilderness today can become beset by doubts and the desire to return to their old lives.

The children of Israel finally arrived on the east side of the Jordan River and pitched camp at a place called Shittim. The Promised Land was within view, but close was not good enough. Remaining on the wrong side of the Jordan proved dangerous. Balak, king of Moab, hired Balaam to curse the Israelites (see Num. 22:39). Balaam was unable to curse God's people, but he told Balak the secret of defeating them, *"Balaam [taught] Balak to put a stumbling block before the sons of Israel, to eat things sacrificed to idols and to commit acts of immorality"* (Rev. 2:14). The results were disastrous:

> *While Israel remained at Shittim, the people began to play the harlot with the daughters of Moab. For they invited the people to the sacrifices of their gods, and the people ate and bowed down to their gods. So Israel joined themselves to Baal of Peor, and the Lord was angry against Israel* (Numbers 25:1-3).

The cost of this dalliance, so close to the Promised Land, was high. Israel incurred God's wrath. As a result, many who were involved in this spiritual adultery lost their lives; and some leaders of the congregation were executed (Num. 25:1-9).

Numbers 33:49-51 adds important details about Israel's campsite; it actually stretched from a place called Beth-jeshimoth to Abel-shittim (Shittim's full name). The meaning of the names of these places is instructive. *Beth-jeshimoth* means "house of wastes."[3] *Abel-shittim* means "mourning of thorns."[4] After the disastrous delay at this inhospitable place, Israel must have been intent on crossing the Jordan. We also must have a level of dissatisfaction with where we are before we will move forward. *Have you lived among the waste and thorns long enough?* Are you ready for the Promised Land?

God had better things in store for His people than Egypt, the wilderness life, or camping close to, but oh so far from, the "milk and honey" land of Israel. This new generation of Israelites stood on the precipice of a God-given choice—remaining in nomadic slavery to self until they also died or following Joshua into the Land of Promise. It was the seeming safety of the seen and known, as uncomfortable and dangerous as it might be, versus the risk of faith and change. None of that generation of Israelites had seen the land. They had to trust God's Word, and the witness of Joshua and Caleb, that what was ahead greatly surpassed Egyptian servitude, the dry wilderness, and their present camp.

God commanded, *"This book of the law shall not depart from your mouth, but you shall meditate on it day and night....then you will make your way prosperous, and then you will have success"* (Josh. 1:8). Joshua—and the millions who followed him—got **direction from the Word of God** (Component #3). They applied the Word and thus experienced success. It will be the same for us. Only by regularly hearing the voice of God will we have the courage to do God's will and overcome the fear of giants.

Israel had changed; it was no longer a ragtag assembly composed of competing factions existing in the wilderness. They now shared a common vision and commitment. God had forged them into a determined, **unified** army (Component #4) that would not be denied the victory. Similarly, *a local church must have a transforming sense of togetherness and purpose to move boldly toward revival.*

Israel **demonstrated obedience to God-ordained human authority** (Component #5) by quickly obeying the commands issued by Joshua. The directions were passed along a chain of command:

> *Joshua commanded the officers of the people, saying, "Pass through the midst of the camp and command the people, saying, 'Prepare provisions for yourselves, for within three days you are to cross this*

Jordan, to go in to possess the land which the Lord your God is giving you'" (Joshua 1:10-11).

In other words, get yourself together and get ready to go forward. The next command was to the Reubenites, Gadites, and the half tribe of Manasseh, who had taken their inheritance on the east side of the Jordan River. Joshua commanded them to, *"Cross before your brothers...and help them"* (Josh. 1:14). This imperative was directed to those who already possessed their inheritance. This illustrates that those who walk in victory need to assist others to do the same.

The people accepted Joshua's leadership and pledged obedience. They wanted an anointed leader and were ready to enforce obedience to that leader among themselves:

> *All that you have commanded us we will do, and wherever you send us we will go. Just as we obeyed Moses in all things, so we will obey you; only may the Lord your God be with you as He was with Moses. Anyone who rebels against your command and does not obey your words in all that you command him, shall be put to death; only be strong and courageous* (Joshua 1:16-18).

Moses had been the recognized leader, and now the mantle of leadership passed to Joshua. We do not see the people grumbling or complaining as they went forward. The Israelites illustrated well the powerful principle of obedience to God-ordained leadership. Too often we sacrifice this important component in the revival protocol to our independent spirit.

The Israelites were on the verge of entering the Promised Land—a life-changing experience for each of them. They would not return to Egypt, nor would they continue to wander in the wilderness. However, entrance to the land was blocked by the Jordan River in flood stage. They had no idea how they were going to cross it, but they put their trust in Joshua to lead them forward. His direction at this point was, *"Consecrate your-selves* (Component #14), *for tomorrow the Lord will do wonders among you"* (Josh. 3:5). In the same way there may seem to be an impenetrable barrier between us and true revival. The lesson for us is clear. When we have gone as far as we can go and the way is blocked, we must give ourselves completely to Jesus and trust Him to do something wonderful.

Understanding the principle of consecration is very important.[5] Although it is not specifically mentioned in every revival, it is evident that consecration is part and parcel of every move of God. To consecrate something means to set it apart to God, to no longer use it for something else. The Jewish nation had come to the doorstep of Canaan, but the dust of the wilderness still rested upon their garments. Joshua's command to consecrate themselves meant the Israelites were to give themselves to God. We are also commanded to separate ourselves from the world and give ourselves to God. John, the apostle, said,

> Do not love the world nor the things in the world. If anyone loves the world, the love of the Father is not in him. For all that is in the world, the lust of the flesh and the lust of the eyes and the boastful pride of life, is not from the Father, but is from the world (1 John 2:15-16).

Consecration symbolizes the end of life lived according to the desires and dictates of the world. It is the beginning of, or recommitment to, life lived according to the desires and dictates of God. Consecration means death to worldly and "wilderness" living.

The people of Israel were at the banks of the *Jordan*, which means "descender." They stayed there for three days, giving us a picture of the grave (Josh. 3:1; Esther 4:16; Matt. 12:40). The Jordan runs below sea level as it approaches the Dead Sea, the lowest point on earth. This river illustrates humbling ourselves and dying to the works and attitudes of the flesh, which Paul tells us are: *"immorality, impurity, sensuality, idolatry, sorcery, enmities, strife, jealousy, outbursts of anger, disputes, dissensions, factions, envying, drunkenness, carousing, and things like these"* (Gal. 5:19-21). All these things must be jettisoned from our lives and left on the "east bank of the Jordan."

Joshua said, *"Consecrate yourselves for tomorrow the Lord will do wonders among you"* (Josh. 3:5). Like the Israelites, we choose to consecrate our-selves—not only because of what the Lord has done, but in anticipation of what He *will do* in our lives. Specifically, we can anticipate that *He will stop the waters of the Jordan and miraculously make a way for us to cross into the Promised Land* of abundance and victory.

If your vision is to succeed spiritually, there comes a time when you must intentionally set out from where you are, determined to become what you want to be (see Josh. 3:1). Those who enter the "Promised Land" of revival are tired of the world's ways, tired of living in the wilderness among waste and thorns, tired enough to get up and **move forward** (Component #19). Joshua encouraged the wilderness-weary people by reminding them of God's promise:

> *By this you shall know that the living God is among you and that He will assuredly dispossess from before you the Canaanite... Behold, the ark of the covenant of the Lord of all the earth is crossing over ahead of you into the Jordan* (Joshua 3:10-11).

They took this encouragement of victory to heart and boldly followed the Lord as the Ark of the Covenant showed the way.

STAGE TWO REVIVAL (GOD RETURNS TO HIS PEOPLE)

An amazing miracle occurred (revival protocol *result* #1).[6] The nation's spiritual preparation and consecration was an open invitation to the Lord to act. As the priests carrying the Ark of the Covenant entered the Jordan River a stupendous miracle took place:

> *The waters which were flowing down from above stood and rose up in one heap, a great distance away at Adam, the city that is beside Zarethan; and those which were flowing down toward the sea of the Arabah, the Salt Sea, were completely cut off so the people crossed opposite Jericho* (Joshua 3:15-16).

The waters of the Jordan piled up and waited obediently while a nation of at least two and a half million people crossed over into Canaan land.

Note that some brave individuals had to trust Joshua enough to pick up and carry the Ark of the Lord into the flooded river. Some had to be in that lead group. They were Levites and priests—servant leaders. They stood confidently in the river bed while the nation safely walked past them. The need for consecrated "presence bearers" still exists today.

The sons of Israel crossed the Jordan, fully expecting to conquer the land quickly. However, ahead of them lay the intimidating walled city of Jericho, not to mention some giants and the rest of Canaan. God promised His people victory, but they were not ready. As night fell, they pitched their tents on a plain near Jericho, a place that came to be known as Gilgal. There they would erect the Tabernacle and reside for the next 14 years while the land was conquered and apportioned. In Gilgal they would deepen their relationship with God in a transforming way and prepare for victory. Gilgal became crucially important to the Israelites as a center of worship and a base of operations.

We also need a "base camp." We, too, have been promised spiritual victory but like the Israelites, we need to be transformed and prepared for the coming battles. *Gilgal should be a well-known name and place for Christians*, but regrettably, it is not. We must not run past spiritual Gilgal in our zeal to take down the strongholds ahead of us. If we do, we will see little victory. The Church needs to learn about Gilgal and experience what I call the 12 Rs of Gilgal.

THE TWELVE RS OF GILGAL

1. Gilgal is the place of *Remembrance*.

   From the riverbed, a dozen preselected men each carried a stone to their camp. There they stacked these 12 stones as a memorial so that all Israel would remember the miracle-working power of the Lord who brought them into the Promised Land. They needed to remember what God had done. Joshua told the Israelites that stopping the Jordan was just as the Lord "had done to the Red Sea," and that it was a reminder that *"the hand of the Lord is mighty, so that you may fear the Lord your God forever"* (Josh. 4:24).

   We also must remember the miraculous hand of God in our lives. We must remember that God not only saves us and delivers us from slavery to sin, but that He makes a way for us to enter a land flowing with spiritual milk and honey. *This will give us courage to encircle the strongholds and face the giants.*

2. Gilgal is the place of *Renunciation* of the flesh.

   The children of Israel had crossed the river, but God commanded circumcision as a symbol of their renunciation of the practices of the worldly kingdom and the rebellious ways of the wilderness (see Josh. 5:2). None of the men born in the wilderness had been circumcised, a requirement for all male descendants of Abraham. Circumcision was more than an initiation ritual or badge of membership. It was the mark of God's Kingdom—signifying the circumcised man lived under God's authority and by His rules. Through circumcision, the

Israelites rejected the culture of Egypt and chose to live under God's lordship.

Today, the circumcision required by the Lord is that of the heart, not the body. This spiritual surgery is required for God's people because it marks the inner, rather than the outer, man. The Scriptures reveal that it has always been God's desire to circumcise this inner man.

The Lord your God will circumcise your heart and the heart of your descendants, to love the Lord your God with all your heart and with all your soul, in order that you may live (Deuteronomy 30:6).

He is not a Jew who is one outwardly; nor is circumcision that which is outward in the flesh. But he is a Jew who is one inwardly; and circumcision is that which is of the heart (Romans 2:28-29).

After circumcision, the Lord's message to Israel through Joshua was, *"Today I have rolled away the reproach of Egypt from you"* (Josh. 5:9). When those in the Church live in an ungodly manner, they are a reproach to God. When we circumcise our hearts and renounce our fleshly ways and accept God's rule over us, He removes this reproach from us.

Circumcision represents submission of the most intimate part of our lives to the Lord. It means we hold nothing back from the Lord. It says, in effect, "God, cut away my flesh." Some of us need to submit to this spiritual knife; we must let "Doctor Y'shua" operate on us, for this open-heart surgery can only be done by Him. Colossians 2:11 states, *"In Him you were also*

*circumcised with a circumcision made without hands, in the removal
of the body of the flesh by the circumcision of Christ."*

The cutting away of self is a painful process and will require
a time of healing (see Josh. 5:8). Yet, this surgery must take
place before we can go on to win victories. Do not be afraid
of the Spirit's knife; it brings freedom. If we are unwilling
to renounce the flesh, we carry the reproach of Egypt, and
that is spiritually dangerous. Paul talks about those who used
to walk with the Lord but now are enemies of the cross of
Christ. "[Their] *god is their appetite, and their glory is in their
shame,* [they] *set their minds on earthly things"* (Phil. 3:18-19).
These one-time believers apparently had not experienced a
deep circumcision of the heart.

When God first commanded circumcision establishing
covenant relationship with Abraham (see Gen. 17:1-3), He
gave Abraham some significant promises. The Lord said to
Abraham, *"You will be a father"* (Gen. 17:4-7). Circumcision
does not destroy our ability to produce life. On the contrary,
it enables us to be a conduit for true life. He also promised
him *"the land of Canaan for an everlasting possession"* (Gen. 17:8).
God's gift of the land to Abraham and his descendants was
directly associated with circumcision. Circumcision of the
heart is still required today to gain our spiritual inheritance.

3. Gilgal is the place of restored *Relationship.*

*"While the sons of Israel camped at Gilgal, they observed the **Passover**
(Result #10) on the evening of the fourteenth day of the month on
the desert plains of Jericho"* (Josh. 5:10). They had not celebrated
Passover since Israel camped at Mount Sinai. In the years that
followed, they had wandered pointlessly in the wilderness.
The application is clear: we cannot feast on the Lord when

our hearts are rebellious or doubting. However, immediately after submitting to spiritual circumcision—the cutting away of fleshly desires—we experience a renewed relationship and closeness to the Lord.

I love the fact that Israel was camped on the plains of Jericho, under the watchful eyes of their enemies. This is a truth that David immortalized in the 23rd Psalm, *"You prepare a table before me in the presence of my enemies"* (Ps. 23:5). This was also a significant day of the year: the fourteenth day of Nisan. This was the day Noah opened the Ark. It was also the day an angel would roll away the stone from a tomb in Jerusalem.

4. Gilgal is the place of *Reaping*.

On the day after the Passover, they ate some of the produce of the land, unleavened cakes and parched grain. The manna ceased the next day (see Josh. 5:11-12). Bread from Heaven was great, but Israel had to learn to bring in the harvest. They would learn and be more involved in the process of growing and gathering food. God's people had been spoon-fed for a generation. Now God was requiring more responsibility from them. For us, it illustrates the Lord's expectation that when you cross the Jordan you must mature and be able to feed yourself spiritually. It also represents bringing in the spiritual harvest that will be available to us in the Promised Land.

5. Gilgal is the place of *Revelation*.

Joshua met the Captain of the Host at Gilgal (see Josh. 5:13-6:5). After the preparation of circumcision, Passover, and partaking of the produce of the land, Joshua had an amazing experience. He saw a man with a drawn sword. Joshua asked him, *"Are you for us or for our adversaries?"* The warrior replied, *"No; rather I indeed come now as captain of the host of the Lord."*

Joshua bowed and **worshiped** (Result #2) the one with the drawn sword and said, *"What has my Lord to say to his servant?"* (Josh. 5:13-14). The visitor did two things:

- He declared Gilgal to be holy ground, demanding that Joshua remove his sandals (see Josh. 5:15).

- He revealed a plan of attack on the Canaanite stronghold of Jericho (see Josh. 6:1-5).

We also need to worship the Lord before spiritual battles for strongholds, find ourselves on holy ground, and affirm our allegiance to the Captain of the Host. In addition, we desperately need direction on how to proceed in battle. God often has a unique and creative plan for bringing the strongholds down. *This kind of revelatory experience readies us for the conflicts to come,* giving us confidence and faith that with the Captain of the Host we can overcome whatever might lie ahead.

We also read that *"Abram passed through the land as far as the site of Shechem, to the oak of Moreh...*(which are "opposite Gilgal," see Deut. 11:30) *and the Lord appeared to Abram and said, 'To your descendants I will give this land'"* (Gen. 12:6-7). God will reveal Himself and His plan where people move forward at His direction.

Moses commanded that a complete reading of the Pentateuch be done when Joshua and the children of Israel entered the land. You may recall reading about this great event conducted between Mount Gerizim and Mount Ebal (see Josh. 8:32-34). Consider where these two mountains are located—*"opposite Gilgal, beside the oaks of Moreh"* (Deut. 11:29-31).

We should also take note that later the school of the prophets was established at Gilgal (see 2 Kings 4:38). Those who would prophesy for the Lord today can learn much in this spiritual, holy place of revelation.

6. 7. and 8. Gilgal is the place of *Reproof, Reconsecration, and Redirection.*

Achan's thievery at Jericho, which had been dedicated to the Lord as first fruits of the land (see Josh. 7:1), created the situation for the next three *Rs*. Because of sin in the camp, Israel lacked the Lord's support when they attempted to conquer Ai, the next city (see Josh. 7:11-12). In addition, Israel apparently grew overconfident after they defeated Jericho. There is no record of Joshua seeking the Lord for direction about how to proceed. As a result, the assault on Ai failed and they lost 36 men in the process (see Josh. 7:2-5). The defeat was disastrous for morale (see Josh. 7:5). Joshua and the elders entered an overly dramatic time of repentance (see Josh. 7:6-9) to which God responded somewhat surprisingly with a reproof, "Rise up! Why is it that you have fallen on your face?" (Josh. 7:10). In other words, *"Get up and set things right."* This illustrates that the Church can lament over our defeats, but unless we are ready to remove blatant sin from our midst, we will have a tenuous hold on the Promised Land of victory.

The Lord demanded a fresh consecration and proceeded to tell Joshua how to deal with the Achan situation (see Josh. 7:11-15). The people reconsecrated themselves and the unrepentant offender was removed (see Josh. 7:16-26).

Once this situation was dealt with, God immediately gave fresh direction to Joshua on how to proceed against Ai (see Josh. 8:1-2), which was quickly overcome (see Josh. 8:3-29).

The Achan/Ai experience provides a powerful example of the need to keep any revival holy. A move of God is not for personal profit. Greed and selfishness can derail, or at least postpone, victory and cause great loss. In addition, there is a warning note here about proceeding without direction. When God stops speaking to us about how to go forward, a red flag should be raised until we seek Him and correct any problem.

9. Gilgal is the place from which Israel *Responded* to attack.

After their victories at Jericho and Ai, the Israelites responded to a plea for help from the Gibeonites. They were under attack because they had made peace with Israel. *"Joshua went up from Gilgal, he and all the people of war with him and all the valiant warriors"* (Josh. 10:9). They came upon the enemy army surrounding Gibeon by marching all night from Gilgal. If we are spiritually camped at Gilgal, we are properly prepared to fight spiritual battles. We can march suddenly and effectively on the foe under Jesus' leadership.

10. Gilgal is the place of *Rest*.

Gilgal was the place to which the children of God repeatedly returned after victory (see Josh. 10:15-43). Here they could enjoy their God-given victories, recuperate, and gain strength. We, too, need to return to holy ground after battle to rejoice and be refreshed.

11. Gilgal is the place of **Receiving a promised inheritance** (Result #10).

Gilgal was where Caleb approached Joshua to claim his long-deferred inheritance. Joshua 14:6-15 tells how the tribe of Judah stood before Joshua in Gilgal at the time for apportionment of the land. The oldest one among them had patiently waited for the inheritance promised to him 45 years before. Caleb, 85 years old but strong and capable, said, *"'Now then, give me this hill country about which the Lord spoke on that day....' So Joshua blessed him, and gave Hebron to Caleb the son of Jephunneh for an inheritance"*(Josh. 14:12-13). Spiritually, Gilgal is the place where, by faith, we approach our Joshua (Jesus) and receive our promised inheritance. This inheritance could mean a place of ministry, financial blessing, peace, fellowship with Him, or other promise of God.

12. Gilgal is the place of *Renewal*.

• When God's people suffered defeat at Ai, they came back to Gilgal and received fresh direction from the Lord. Similarly, when our hearts are crushed in spiritual battle, or we experience a dramatic reversal or loss, we can come back to Gilgal and say, God you brought us into this land. What would you have us do?

• Gilgal is where the message and call to revival is nurtured and brought forth. In Judges chapter 2, the children of Israel again needed to return to the Lord. We read that the Angel of the Lord *"came up from Gilgal"*(Judg. 2:1). He spoke two things to the people. First was a comforting word: *"I brought you up out of Egypt and led you into the land which I have sworn to your fathers; and I said, 'I will never break My covenant with you.'"* But He also spoke rebuke:

"[I told you to] *make no covenant with the inhabitants of this land; you shall tear down their altars. But you have not obeyed Me; what is this you have done?"...When the angel of the Lord spoke these words to all the sons of Israel, the people lifted up their voices and wept* (Judges 2:2-4).

If we are to experience true revival, we must not only hear the comforting Word of the Lord to us, but we must also embrace His rebuke, and weep over our disobedience. May the "Angel of the Lord" come up from Gilgal and speak to us also.

Four hundred years later, Samuel said to Israel, *"Come and let us go to Gilgal and renew the kingdom there"* (1 Sam. 11:14). He must have been reading the Book of Joshua at the time. It is time for us to go to Gilgal and renew the Kingdom.

Following the time of preparation at Gilgal, **a miraculous victory** ensued (Result #1). The walls of Jericho fell before Israel. This was a crushing defeat for the Canaanites. The most formidable of their walled cities was reduced to rubble and its population was totally destroyed (see Josh. 6:20).

Typical of all revivals, organized aggressive **opposition** (Result #15) arose to counter this great advance by God's people. Resistance is the response of the enemy's kingdom to revival and victory in God's camp:

> When all the kings who were beyond the Jordan, in the hill country and in the lowland and on all the coast of the Great Sea toward Lebanon, the Hittite and the Amorite, the Canaanite, the Perizzite, the Hivite and the Jebusite, heard of it (the defeat of Jericho), they gathered themselves together with one accord to fight with Joshua and with Israel (Joshua 9:1-2).

Shrewd and deceitful attempts to subvert and compromise the work also take place as evidenced by the Gibeonite fiasco:

> When the inhabitants of Gibeon heard what Joshua had done to Jericho and to Ai, they also acted craftily and set out as envoys, and took worn-out sacks on their donkeys, and wineskins worn-out and torn and mended, and worn-out and patched sandals on

their feet, and worn-out clothes on themselves; and all the bread of their provision was dry and had become crumbled. They went to Joshua to the camp at Gilgal and said to him and to the men of Israel,"We have come from a far country; now therefore, make a covenant with us"(Joshua 9:3-6).

We must be prepared for warfare when we return to God and pursue revival. Let not our faith, obedience, and wisdom fail, for God has promised us the land.

REVIVAL THEME

The Joshua revival teaches us we must leave the wilderness and enter the Promised Land. Rather than wander short of the goal or remain encamped at Abel-Shittim God's people decided to cross the Jordan. A strong desire to advance into the destiny promised by the Lord and actually crossing whatever barrier is in the way is critically important if there is to be revival. God stopped the Jordan in flood tide long enough for at least two and a half million people to cross. This initial miracle enabled the Israelites to enter the Promised Land. It must have made them giddy with joy and excitement. We could understand had they rushed forward to try to conquer Jericho at this point. However, we should take note of the time of renewing and deepening their relationship with the Lord at Gilgal before advancing to take down the stronghold that lay before them. *Gilgal is the great secret of the Joshua revival.* This base camp was where preparation took place that enabled the ensuing victories in the Promised Land.

ENDNOTES

1. A narrative based on Joshua 6.

2. Numbering of revival protocol components corresponds to Table 1 on pages 24 and 25.

3. Matthew G. Easton, *Easton's Bible Dictionary,* (Nashville, TN: Thomas Nelson, 1897).

4. Roswell D. Hitchcock, *Hitchcock's Bible Names Dictionary* (Austin, TX: WORD*search* Corp. 1869).

5. Chapter 8 contains a more extensive discussion of consecration.

6. The numbers used to identify the results of returning to God correspond to Table 2 on pages 26 and 27.

POINTS TO PONDER

1. Contrast the characteristics of "wilderness living" with life in the Promised Land.

2. Israel was finally ready to enter the Promised Land but they faced the Jordan in flood stage, a great barrier to entering the land of Canaan. What sort of barriers might a church face when poised on the border of God's promised land of victory?

3. The barrier of the Jordan was breached by some brave individuals the author describes as "presence bearers." What was their key job, and what were the results?

4. The author states that "the great secret of the Joshua revival is Gilgal." What does he mean by this, and why is this critically important stop on the Israelites' journey so little known?

5. Of the 12 *Rs* of Gilgal, which 3 would you consider most important?

Chapter 3

The Samuel Revival
When You Are Tired of
Life Without God

Victory at the Old Watchtower[1]

The tower had stood on the rise longer than anyone could remember. Built of rough-hewn fieldstone, it overlooked the gently rolling landscape a few miles north west of Jerusalem. It was called *Mizpah,* or "watchtower." All Israel had assembled there at Samuel's direction. Frustrated by years of Philistine domination and oppression, the people had earlier sent a delegation asking the man of God what to do. Samuel, last and greatest of Israel's judges, commanded them to destroy their pagan idols and serve the Lord. If they would do so, he promised he would pray for them at Mizpah. With their idols pulverized, tens of thousands came to the old tower to return to the Lord God. The men carried their weapons for fear of the Philistines, since Israel's arch enemy habitually raided the Hebrew farms and villages at harvest time, stealing crops and terrorizing the towns.

During the first day at Mizpah, Samuel exhorted the nation to return to the Lord with all their hearts, and they responded by fasting and praying. Across the fields around the old tower, groups of broken-hearted people prayed for deliverance and confessed their sins to the Lord. Longstanding disputes between individuals and families were settled. Some issues required Samuel's authoritative wisdom to resolve.

At dusk, the Israelites solemnly drew water from a small spring near the tower and poured it out before the Lord. In so doing, the people gave themselves to God. Nightfall found them breaking their fast. Unity was restored as they sang and talked around campfires in the beautiful late summer air. The people embraced a newfound hope and joy. They talked with excited expectation of God's blessings of liberty, safety, and prosperity being restored.

The second day at Mizpah dawned bright and warm, with preparations to offer a burnt offering for the nation. The stone altar that stood at the foot of the tower needed to be repaired so it was lovingly tended to. Wood was then brought for the fire, and a suckling lamb was selected and brought near. Samuel then instructed the priests to light the fire. He thought gratefully, *The years of prayer for this nation are finally yielding fruit.* A spark was struck and caught on mounded dry stubble. Everyone somberly watched as twigs and then larger limbs were added to the sacrificial fire. Flames flared and crackled. The lamb did not struggle when Samuel lifted it in his strong hands. Cradling the lamb and bowing his head, *he could smell the little animal's clean fragrance and feel the tiny heartbeat against his own chest.* The innocence and vulnerability of a sacrificial lamb always moved him. He never really enjoyed performing such sacrifices, but he knew they were necessary. Samuel paused, thinking, *How amazing, Lord, You cover our sin with the blood of a Lamb.* He felt tears well up in his eyes and one fall unbidden from his cheek onto the soft wool. Looking up, the old prophet saw tears flowing on other faces as well.

Samuel drew the knife and was about to sacrifice the lamb when a commotion began at the far edge of the crowd. A man pushed his way through the crowd, shouting that a large army of Philistines was encamped just over the rise. This news electrified the atmosphere, as fear rapidly replaced hope and peace. Watchmen raced up the tower. Men checked their weapons. Some people wanted to flee. The agitated crowd pleaded with Samuel, "Pray that the Lord will have mercy and save us!" Still holding the lamb, Samuel spoke confidently, "The Lord will deliver us from the Philistines!" Out of respect for the man of God, they quieted themselves quickly. Samuel's dark eyes were serious and intent as he spoke, "Let us make the sacrifice." Everyone nodded.

A breeze bent the grass around the altar as Samuel lifted the lamb aloft while calling on the Lord—it was a simple prayer asking for mercy and help. As Samuel's words faded, the heavens rumbled; some who were there that day said words spoken in the thunder replied to Samuel's prayer. Samuel laid the lamb down but held him still. The knife stroke was quick. Red drops splattered here and there, coloring the altar stones scarlet and wetting the ground. Blood also stained Samuel's robe as he laid the small body on the fire which was now hot. Lamb's wool and skin sizzled. The prophet stood tall in the swirling smoke, hands raised, while everyone cried out to the Lord.

In spite of the prayer, or maybe because of it, a trembling shout rang out from the watchmen on the tower. "They're coming! They're coming!" Indeed, the Philistines were seen advancing across the open landscape brandishing their weapons and shouting their war cries. No doubt, they expected the Israelites to scatter and run, just as they had on many other occasions, but something was different today. The thunder sounded again from the sky growing dark with gathering clouds. Instead of turning to run, the Israelites closed ranks. The advancing Philistines suddenly slowed, surprised, now unsure of what to do. Many of Israel's enemies noticed the cloud of smoke rising above the old watchtower and the tall old man near the stone altar. The Philistine advance sputtered to a halt. For several tense moments, Israel and the invaders stared at each other across the sloping field that separated them.

The brief stalemate was broken when Samuel himself drew a sword and began striding purposefully toward the enemy. The men around him followed Samuel's leadership. *Like an avalanche ominously gathering speed, the men of Israel began to advance toward their stalled foes.*

This turn of events caused even more confusion among the Philistines. Confident aggression degenerated into murmuring insecurity. They straggled into a defensive posture, spears protruding, but from the skies the thunder came again, louder this time, booming in fury above the Philistine formation. Again and again the thunder rolled, somehow focused on the marauders, a sound so loud they couldn't hear their own startled shouts. Some fell to the ground covering their ears; others cowered where they stood. Lightening flashed through the clouds as the stunning explosions of sound continued.

The Israelites were running to the battle now. Courage replaced fear as they realized the Lord was fighting for them. Unbidden, a shout of victory rose in unison from their lips. The Philistines also began to run, not toward the battle but away from it, dropping their weapons as they fled. Israel hotly pursued their enemies, striking them down as far as Beth-car, miles away.

Later, as the sun was descending on the western hills, the sons of Israel gathered around Samuel where he was resting. As the men assembled, they began giving thanks to the Lord. They sang a song of triumph. Samuel rose to his feet, his eyes falling on a rugged rectangular stone more than three cubits in length. "Stand this rock up!" he commanded. Men struggled to raise the great stone. When it finally stood erect, Samuel proclaimed it "Ebenezer," saying, "Thus far the Lord has helped us." With a great cheer, Israel praised the Lord God for the victory over their persistent enemy, the Philistines.

THE SETTING FOR REVIVAL

Prior to the great Mizpah revival, Israel had been in dire straits. Constant raids and harassment by the Philistines over the years had taken a great toll. Cities and land belonging to the Israelites had been abandoned to the encroaching enemy. Not only did Israel lose property, they lost their passion for God and their grasp of His promise. Worst of all, they lost the Ark of the Covenant. The symbol of God's presence had been captured by the Philistines in battle. Eli, the high priest, had died at the shock of the news. His daughter-in-law, struggling to give birth at the time, named the boy she bore Ichabod, *"the glory has departed"* and then died (1 Sam. 4:21). When the presence of God departs, only death, sorrow, and orphans remain.

The Philistines discovered that the presence of God was nothing to trifle with. They soon returned the Ark to escape the misery it was generating among them. Yet, all was not well in Israel. The Ark of God had been returned to Israel, but Israel had not returned to God. They were spiritually ignorant, having no clue how to approach God. They treated the Ark without proper reverence, and more than 50,000 were struck down by God (see 1 Sam. 6:13-21). As a result, Israel stored the Ark of the Covenant in the house of Abinadab. They may have been fearful to bring it out because they were not sure whether God was for them or against them.

A sad unsatisfying status quo continued year after year. *"The house of Israel lamented after the Lord"* (1 Sam. 7:2), but they did nothing to change the situation. The Philistines continued to harass and dominate them and the Ark remained hidden. God's people were living in sin and worshiping idols. When Israel finally reached the point of desperation, they wanted change badly enough to ask Samuel, the man of God, what the problem was, and what they needed to do about it.

It will be helpful to understand the place that God allowed the Philistines to occupy in relationship to Israel. The Philistines lived primarily in the coastal land of Canaan and constantly fought Israel for dominance of the whole country. This conflict between Israel and the Philistines had started long before Samuel's time. For, when Isaac looked for the wells dug by his father, Abraham, he found they had been filled with dirt by the Philistines (see Gen. 26:14-16). Later, when the Israelites came out of Egypt, God did not lead them along the coastal route toward the Promised Land, even though it was a shorter distance. Why? The Philistines lived there and God said, *"The people might change their minds when they see war, and return to Egypt"* (Exod. 13:16-18). God knew that war was inevitable between His people and the Philistines. This struggle for control of the Promised Land continues today.

There was no quarter given in the ongoing war between Israel and Philistia, and no truce. Even the Philistines knew it was a choice of enslaving the Hebrews or being slaves themselves. When confronted by the army of Israel on another occasion they said to each other, *"Take courage and be men, O Philistines, or you will become slaves to the Hebrews, as they have been slaves to you; therefore, be men and fight"* (1 Sam. 4:9).

The Philistines ruled the land whenever Israel became weak. When God's people were strong the Philistines were driven back and Israel recovered their territory. Samuel knew that God was allowing the Philistines to have victory because Israel had fallen away from the Lord. He knew deliverance would only come if the people returned to the Lord.

We can see that the Philistines, who continued to live within the Promised Land, represent our inner enemy—the flesh, which is the tendency within us to sin. The flesh objects when we take our first step toward the Promised Land and will continue to fight to dominate our lives. Just like the constant opposition by the Philistines against Israel, the flesh always wars against the Spirit.

The Philistines stole the Israelites' inheritance as their devotion to the Lord faltered. In the same way, the flesh steals passion and promise from us when we turn from the Lord. Like Israel, we experience the loss of "cities and lands"—the blessings and victories received from God. The end result of allowing the flesh to gain control is grief over the loss of blessings and a sad longing for the Lord's presence.

Just as the Philistines and Israelites continued to make war on each other, there can be no peaceful coexistence with our carnal nature; *either the Spirit of God will lead us in victory or the flesh will dominate our lives.* When we grow lukewarm and weak in the Lord, we allow the flesh to rule.

Like the Israelites in Samuel's day who longed for victory over the Philistines, Christians today know they are not called to live under the intimidation and power of the flesh. Rather, we must cry out for the answer to our problems. When the command to return to the Lord comes, we must gather at the "watchtower" and pour ourselves out before the Lord. When Israel returned to the Lord, He defeated their archenemy. If we will return to the Lord, God will also give us thunderous victory over our difficult and persistent foe.

STAGE ONE REVIVAL (GOD'S PEOPLE RETURN TO HIM)

Samuel had been raised in the Tabernacle and arose to give **strong godly leadership** (Component #1) to Israel in its time of need. His commitment to prayer and God's Word was deep. He promised the Israelites, *"Far be it from me that I should sin against the Lord by ceasing to pray for you; but I will instruct you in the good and right way"* (1 Sam. 12:23).

Prayerful, Word-centered, prophetic leaders like Samuel are instrumental in achieving and maintaining spiritual victories. They speak into the lives of leaders and pour anointing on them. Samuel took a flask of oil, *"poured it on [Saul's] head, kissed him and said, 'Has not the Lord anointed you a ruler over His inheritance?'"* (1 Sam. 10:1). Later, Samuel also, *"took the horn of oil and anointed* [David] *in the midst of his brothers; and the Spirit of the Lord came mightily upon David from that day forward"* (1 Sam. 16:13).

The prophet-leader is honored by God. *"Samuel judged the sons of Israel"* (1 Sam. 7:6). The position of judge was one of prominence and power. It often takes time, but the prophet-prayer-warrior will eventually be recognized; if not here, certainly in Heaven's courts. It is important to note that this privilege and power were earned through proven character and faithfulness. Samuel displayed the loving heart of God. He was neither arrogant nor manipulative. Beware of those who feel they have license to judge others, as though they were a spiritual magistrate.

Israel lamented and suffered under Philistine domination for 20 years. *Then* Samuel spoke (1 Sam. 7:2-3). Why didn't Samuel speak earlier? Why did he wait for 20 years? Perhaps Israel needed to lament over their waywardness. Sometimes we need a season of lamenting until we realize how much we need reviving. We know it was the right time for Samuel to speak up because Israel was ready to listen. They wanted to hear the answer to their dilemma.

Samuel yearned for Israel to return to the Lord and break free from the sway of the Philistines. **The people eventually followed their godly leader's vision** (Component #2) and pursued freedom as well. Samuel knew what to say when Israel asked for direction. With wisdom and boldness garnered in the prayer closet, the prophet declared that God would deliver them from the hand of the Philistines. However, this promise came with spiritual conditions. Deliverance would come if they would do four things based on Scripture (Component #3):

1. *Return to the Lord with **all** your heart* (1 Samuel 7:3).

   Half-hearted repentance never works! Real repentance requires us to deal with our divided hearts. Samuel was echoing Deuteronomy 6:5, *"You shall love the Lord your God with all your heart and with all your soul and with all your might."* Let us put aside other passions and love the Lord with everything within us.

2. *Remove the foreign gods and the Ashtaroth from among you* (1 Samuel 7:3).

People in every revival make plain which deity they worship. God had commanded, *"You shall have no other gods before Me"* (Exod. 20:3). Jesus said we cannot serve two masters (see Matt. 6:24). We must serve one God and remove the influence and symbols of all others.

3. *Direct your hearts to the Lord* (1 Samuel 7:3).

Samuel again referenced Moses who said, *"Turn to the Lord your God with all your heart and soul"* (Deut. 30:10). By an act of our will, we can choose and nurture a genuine desire for God.

4. *Serve Him alone* (1 Samuel 7:3).

Samuel's fourth condition was that the Israelites practically labor for the Lord, *"You shall...serve Him"* (Deut. 13:4). In other words, get busy for the Lord. Bend every effort to furthering His kingdom.

Israel responded to Samuel's reproof by **demonstrating obedience to human authority** (Component #5). When we obey the scriptural direction of godly leaders, great things happen. Israel's initial steps of obedience triggered another command: to come together at the old watchtower. Several significant things then occurred at Mizpah.

- Israel came to Mizpah with a purpose of **gaining unity** (Component #4). Israel not only wanted Samuel to pray for them for deliverance from the Philistines, they wanted him to "judge" them (see 1 Sam. 7:5-6). They knew that coming together in the presence of the judge would mean that conflicts among them would be settled. *When we are hungry for renewal, Jesus directs us in a flow of grace and forgiveness that resolves division.*

- **They prayed together** (Component #7). The watchtower is a symbol of prayer. The very name *Mizpah* means "watchtower"; it represents the power of prayer in several ways. From the vantage point of a watchtower, you could locate other workers and members of your family; the condition of the harvest could be ascertained, and in its shade you could rest. In addition, you could see the approach of an attacking force, and once inside the tower, you were safe.

- **They consecrated themselves** (Component #14) at the old tower. Consecration is giving oneself to God, dying to one's own plans and living for Him. At Mizpah the Israelites drew water and poured it out before the Lord (see 1 Sam. 7:6). This act illustrated the willingness to give up one's life as shown in the account of David's mighty men bringing water to him at great risk from the well in Bethlehem (see 2 Sam. 23:16). David refused to drink it. Rather, he poured it out before the Lord, realizing that it represented the lives of his brave men.

- **They fasted** (Component #17) (see 1 Sam. 7:6). Fasting is a powerful discipline that helps us humble ourselves and draw close to the Lord.[2]

- **They confessed their sins** to God (Component #13) (see 1 Sam. 7:6). The people of Israel desperately wanted a new beginning. It was time to publicly admit their shortcomings, receive forgiveness, and demonstrate their firm intention to follow God wholeheartedly.

- They repaired the old altar at Mizpah and **offered a sacrifice** (Component #10) (see 1 Sam. 7:9). Their offering of a suckling lamb provides a beautiful illustration of Jesus as the sacrificial Lamb for all who will come to God repentant, obedient, and prayerful.

When the Philistines heard that the sons of Israel had gathered to Mizpah, they marched there to attack. This illustrates the fact that the flesh objects when you give yourself to the Lord, hunger for more of God, and come to the place of prayer and consecration.

Opposition (Result #15), in one form or another, comes against all revivals. Hezekiah, Jehoshaphat, Asa, and Nehemiah experienced opposition. Jonathan Edwards, the Wesley brothers and the leaders of the Azusa Street Revival could also attest to this pattern. Satan doesn't mind a sleeping Church, but hates and fears an awakening Church and fights against her.

We must not panic when the attack comes. The sons of Israel heard the Philistines were coming against them and were fearful (see 1 Sam. 7:7). Despite their fear, God's people did the right thing: they asked Samuel to keep praying, cried out for help in their crisis, and kept their focus on the sacrificial Lamb (see 1 Sam. 7:8-10). As a result God gave them a great victory.

The prayers didn't stop the attack of the Philistines. In fact, they may have precipitated it. We need to understand that *God often wants us to confront the forces of evil so we can witness the resounding victory He will bring.*

Stage Two Revival (God Returns to His People)

The Philistines were accustomed to winning, but a new dynamic now characterized the struggle with their archenemy. The Philistines mounted an attack, but **a miraculous intervention occurred** (Result #1). The Lord Himself entered the fray in defense of His people. He thundered against the Philistines and so confused them, they were routed before

Israel. The divine sonic attack is described as "a great thunder." In other words, this was not just another summer thunderstorm. The Philistines were thrown into total confusion and disarray by this meteorological phenomenon.

Israel came out of Mizpah, the Lord's stronghold, and defeated the enemy. The victory began as the lamb was being offered up (see 1 Sam. 7:10-11). When we return to the Lord and cry out while lifting up the Lamb, God hears and answers.

The Philistines were subdued during the rest of Samuel's days (see 1 Sam. 7:13). Samuel helped maintain spiritual health in Israel by moving in an annual preaching circuit. It is interesting to note the four places he regularly visited: Bethel, Gilgal, Mizpah, and Ramah (see 1 Sam. 7:16). This illustrates a prophetic circle of ministry based on the truths represented by these sites. Bethel (house of God) is the dwelling place of the Lord. Gilgal (rolling away) represents circumcision of the heart and the rolling away of sin and reproach. Mizpah (watchtower) is the place of prayer and spiritual preparation, and Ramah (a height) is the place of victory.

Praise and worship (Result #2) were lifted to the Lord. Israel gave God the glory for their victory. Samuel erected a memorial at Mizpah lest any in Israel should forget the great triumph. He set up a stone near the watchtower and named it Ebenezer saying, *"Thus far the Lord has helped us"* (see 1 Sam. 7:12).

The cities stolen by the Philistines were restored (Result #5) and **peace returned to Israel** (Result #8) (see 1 Sam. 7:13-14). Israel drove the Philistines out of Beth-car (house of pasture) (see 1 Sam. 7:11). The house of pasture was where the sheep were supposed to be. This victory restored the Israelites' ability to raise their flocks. The application for us centers on driving the enemy out of the Church—our "house of pasture." God restored everything to His people when they returned to Him. Our God is a merciful God. We miss the mark and lose our blessings, our passion, our promise, and the Lord's presence. But when we return to the Lord, He restores us.

REVIVAL THEME

The Samuel revival reveals that God is willing to wait until His people long for His return. The Church must ask itself if it is willing to live under the constant domination of the flesh. It was not until Israel "lamented" after the Lord, sought direction, and made some beginning steps of obedience that the status quo changed. Are we desperate for a change?

ENDNOTES

1. A narrative based on First Samuel 7.

2. Chapter 7 contains a more complete discussion of fasting.

POINTS TO PONDER

1. What parallels do you see between the Philistines and the flesh?

2. What is meant by the phrase "lamenting after the Lord"? Is it a good thing or a bad thing?

3. Why did it take 20 years for this awakening to start? What was the turning point for the people's return to God?

4. What were the key events at the old watchtower that precipitated the Lord's involvement the next time the Philistines attacked?

Chapter 4

The David Revival
Bringing in the Presence of the Lord

David Dances[1]

He strode, jaw clenched, past the guard at the palace door. Uncharacteristically, he did not acknowledge the man's salute. King David's mind was whirling, "How could it have happened? *Why* did it happen? There was no warning! The Lord struck the man dead!" The king's heavy steps echoed loudly on the stone paving of the great hall. He continued angrily down the long tapestry-hung corridor to his living quarters and slammed the door shut behind him as he entered. One of the women came to comfort him, but he waved her away with a scowl. Attendants scurried quietly from the room as they saw his grim mood. Casting his cloak aside, the king threw himself face down on the soft carpet. At first no words came. He finally groaned in shock and sorrow, "Oh Lord, *why?*" David lay awaiting an explanation until the sun went down, but the heavens were silent.

The day was supposed to have been a crowning achievement. Wounds from Saul's paranoid leadership had at last started to heal; the northern alliance of tribes had joined Judah in accepting the son of Jesse's leadership (David was still amazed that the Lord had made him king of all Israel). Jerusalem, the new capital, hummed with construction and energy. The army had successfully routed the Philistine threat and this day was to have been a great day. Hurt and confusion welled up. David inwardly groaned again. He rolled over, his eyes searching the darkened room, even as his mind was searching for an answer.

Despite the disastrous results, things had started out well that morning. The plans were momentous. After years of yearning and much preparation, the time had arrived to bring the Ark of the Covenant to the city. *Above its solid gold mercy seat and between the out stretched wings of cherubim dwelt the heavenly Majesty.* David had anticipated that by nightfall all Israel would be worshiping before the very presence of the Lord God Himself. Leaving Jerusalem early that morning, he had driven his chariot to the place just outside the city where Gihon, the beautiful spring that supplied the city of David with water, flowed from the shoulder of Mount Zion. He had inspected the large tent that stood beside the clear burbling water. The magnificent Ark would reside here, at the Tabernacle of David, until the Temple could be built.

By the time David arrived at Kiriath-jearim, 30,000 Israelites were gathered and the day was already warm. At his command, men lifted the Ark of the Mighty One of Israel. Using long poles passed through the solid gold rings on its sides, they struggled to carry it out of Abinadab's house where it had rested for more than 40 years. Once outside, the men lowered the heavy Ark onto the cushioned planks of a newly made oxcart. Abinadab's sons Ahio and Uzzah proudly guided the huge pair of oxen as the procession started toward the city. Wooden wheels found their way awkwardly in rutted tracks. The orchestra of harps, lyres, tambourines, trumpets, and cymbals struck up a song of praise. David celebrated with the massive throng and admired the gleaming cargo. Excited onlookers followed and filled the grassy verges of the country road. The cart trundled along smoothly enough...until they reached the place called Chidon's threshing floor. That's when disaster struck.

David saw the whole thing as though it happened in slow motion. In the little hollow, where rain had washed out the edge of what passed for a road, the right-hand wheels dipped suddenly and, for a moment, the Ark swayed. Golden wings leaned precipitously. The oxen pulling up the rise added to the strain and, for a horrible moment, David thought the Ark would crash to the ground. Ahio, at the head of the team, could not see the impending disaster, but his brother did! Instinctively, Uzzah dropped the ox goad he carried and reached for the Ark. He held on to the corner of the gold-clad chest, perhaps thinking he would steady it for the remainder of the trip. Only time for a single breath and then—with awful fury—a bolt of energy crackled from between the cherubim; its blue deadly power was obvious. So devastating and lethal was the strike on Uzzah that even David's 30 mighty men marching immediately behind the cart fell back. It was over in an instant; Uzzah lay on the ground lifeless. *Acrid smoke assaulted David's nostrils as in shock he approached and knelt beside the man.* Gray clouds had gathered unnoticed. They now seemed a fitting shroud for the former festive celebration. Uzzah was gently carried away. The long poles were again gingerly inserted into the gold rings of the Ark by trembling men who carefully carried it to the nearby house of Obed-edom. No one touched it. Few even dared look at it as the crowd dispersed.

David finally rose disconsolate from the floor of his chamber to sit brooding. "Lord, we were doing the right thing. You want the Ark here." David was sure of it. "O Lord, why?" It just didn't make sense. David knew the Lord's desire for Jerusalem and longed for the day when all would come to the city to worship. But now fear and anger clutched at him. "How can I bring the Ark here?" Something was horribly wrong. Frustration festered in his heart throughout the night.

They buried Uzzah with honors the next day; King David had no answers or comfort for his grieving family, except his own grief. The whole nation was in trauma. The God they longed to worship suddenly seemed dangerous and distant.

It was a crisp early morning almost three months later when a thought stirred in David's mind, something he had read long before. He had not slept much of late, tossing and turning, fretting, often rising to pace while the stars were bright. But now hope began to beckon faintly. He threw on a robe and ran barefoot through the palace in the dawn light until he reached the guard room. Three men rose to attention as the king burst in. David commanded, "Send for Abiathar and the Book of the Law!" The youngest soldier scurried out the door, headed for the house of the high priest.

The sun had risen above the Mount of Olives when Abiathar and Zadok entered the palace carrying the scrolls. David told them what he was looking for. The priests took turns reading the words of Moses out loud. It was almost noon when they found the passage about transporting the Ark. The instructions were amazingly clear: the Ark could *only* be carried by poles on consecrated shoulders. David's relief and joy were tempered by a stab of icy conviction. He finally understood the problem, but realized that Uzzah had died needlessly. "How could I have failed to research the God-given method for moving the Ark?" he thought to himself. He wanted to shout at the priests, "Why didn't you say something? Didn't you know?" But their stricken faces and downcast eyes told the story. The three men knelt together and poured out their hearts in repentance and sorrow. They prayed, ignoring the noon meal. Finally, David picked up his lyre from where it had lain idle for some months and began to strum a song. These leaders of Israel worshiped, and peace flooded the room. When they rose, David was whole again.

The Ark would not stay at the house of Obed-edom much longer. David gathered a handful of his captains that night for a critical meeting. Over lamb stew and bread, he shared again his vision to bring the presence of the Lord to Mount Zion. The next day, the king's voice was resolute and confident, while hushed surprise rippled though a larger group of Israel's leaders. They looked at him, incredulous that he planned a second attempt to move the Ark. David turned to some of the oldest in the cedar-paneled room and said, "You are the heads of the households of the Levites. Consecrate yourselves that you may bring up the Ark of the Lord God of Israel to the place that I have prepared for it. Because you didn't carry it, the Lord made an outburst on us (1 Chron. 15:13)." They listened intently as Zadok read the ordinance, nodding as they remembered and understood God's command. As excitement rose among the men, David smiled and whispered, "We want your presence Lord."

At his home near Chidon's threshing floor, Obed-edom stared down at the gourd growing at his feet. He knelt to touch its smooth hard surface. No one in the neighborhood had ever seen one as big. Two others just as large or larger lay in his field. With his sons by his side, Obed-edom stood to survey the wheat bending heavily in the light morning breeze. "Having the Ark here the last three months has changed everything," he said. The boys nodded in agreement and amazement. Jacob, the older, observed, "They'll be here soon to get it." Obed-edom sadly agreed, but his eyes sparkled as they turned to walk toward their house to prepare for their royal visitor. Obed-edom greeted David respectfully on his arrival. The change in the man since David had seen him last was remarkable. No longer bent and sickly, the Gittite radiated a healthy and happy glow. It confirmed what David had heard about the blessing of the Lord resting on Obed-edom's house.

The throng gathering at Obed-edom's farm that day from all Israel was quiet. They had brought from the Tabernacle at Gibeon the large piece of fabric that formed the entrance to the Holy of Holies. A marvel in itself, this veil was beautifully and thickly woven in purple, blue, scarlet, and white. It was the perfect size to wrap the golden angels and chest. Priests entered the house and carefully draped the Ark with the veil, then with a layer of supple leather. Over these they laid a final covering of the finest blue cloth. After they completed their task safely, David breathed a sigh of relief. Twelve linen-clad Levites, sons of Kohath, then entered the house to bring out the Ark. Prayer swelled, hovering over the crowd. Two at a time, holding the poles low, the men began to exit the house. A gasp rose as the second man on the right briefly stumbled, but the Ark, carried by many hands, remained steady. Outside now, muscles strained as the dozen Levites hoisted the massive weight to their shoulders.

In step, those courageous men moved forward, one step, two, then half a dozen paces. They paused while sacrifices were offered. Singers and musicians, also clothed in white, led the way up the road. David's excitement grew, his joy again bubbling. He could sense the pleasure of the Lord. The crowd, surging along behind, felt it as well. Uriel, chief of the Kohathites, told David that his men were saying the Ark now seemed almost weightless. David shouted, *"God Himself is helping us bring the Ark to the city!"* Music and singing swelled in volume and intensity;

worship filled the air. The procession joyfully made their way the remaining few miles to Jerusalem.

City walls soon came into view. People within and without the city were shouting praises to God as the procession drew near. Moving majestically on the shoulders of glad-hearted men, the Ark came to the tent that stood waiting beside the spring just outside Jerusalem's walls. Men, women, and children streamed along toward the place where unending praise would be lifted. Unwilling now to restrain his joy, David began to leap; laying down all kingly reserve and his robes, David began to lead the crowd in passionate worship. Wearing the simple linen ephod, he danced unashamedly and with all his might before the Lord. Immersed in delight David didn't notice the curtain over one of the palace windows suddenly drawn shut.

In the tent, exuberant praise and deep worship continued as appointed teams of musicians and singers began to rotate on an hourly basis. David gave everyone gathered at the tent a kingly gift and blessing.

As the deep velvet Judean night began to engulf the city, many people stayed to enjoy the sweet presence of the Lord. Eventually, David prepared to make his way to the palace. As the gatekeeper drew the tent material aside for the king, David recognized him and asked with surprise, "You're a gatekeeper?" The man replied, "I've moved to Jerusalem. I cannot leave His presence." Smiling, the king said, "I know how it is. Good night, Obed-edom" (1 Chron. 15:24).

THE SETTING FOR REVIVAL

The Israelites had the Ark, but it was stored at the house of Abinadab in Kiriath-jearim. Hidden away, removed from sight and mind, the Ark collected dust and waited for someone to remember. Saul paid no attention to the Ark during his 40-year reign. Instead, he was consumed with a growing jealousy and hatred for his son-in-law David. His paranoid rule was agony for Israel and ended in bloody defeat by the resurgent Philistines.

STAGE ONE REVIVAL (GOD'S PEOPLE RETURN TO HIM)

A strong godly leader arose (Component #1). Following Saul's death, David assumed the throne, but resentment and conflict lingered. One of Saul's generals backed the claim of Saul's son, Ish-bosheth, to be the new king. Only the tribe of Judah accepted David as their king. After seven long years, the kingdom was finally united under David's leadership with Jerusalem as its capital.

The importance of a strong godly leader cannot be overemphasized. Isaiah reveals to us some insight about how the presence of these key individuals affects the health of churches, cities, and nations:

> *Behold, a king will reign righteously and princes will rule justly. Each will be like a refuge from the wind and a shelter from the storm, like streams of water in a dry country, like the shade of a huge rock in a parched land* (Isaiah 32:1-3).

These verses describe the protection and refreshing that a strong godly leader provides. Each stout and righteous leader is like a refuge, a stream, and a rock. Isaiah goes on to express the effects of this strong godly leadership on the populace:

Then the eyes of those who see will not be blinded, and the ears of those who hear will listen. The mind of the hasty will discern the truth, and the tongue of the stammerers will hasten to speak clearly. No longer will the fool be called noble, or the rogue be spoken of as generous (Isaiah 32:4-5).

Eyes will be able to see, ears will be opened, discernment of truth will come, witnesses for the Lord will speak clearly, and people will recognize character correctly.

It is possible to be a strong leader and not be a godly one. It is also possible to be godly without being a strong leader. Every biblical revival was led by a strong leader who was also a humble man whose heart yearned for God. David was such a man; he was not a perfect man. His mid-life moral failure caused untold pain and sorrow to himself, his family, and the nation he led. Nevertheless, he was a determined leader, a warrior, and a true worshiper of God.

David built a palace, consolidated power, and put down an attack by the Philistines. Finally, he was able to focus on a task that was of great importance to him—bringing the Ark of the Covenant to the city. **David gathered and consulted with leadership** (Component #18). He told the leaders of his plan to get the Ark of the Covenant that had been hidden for so long. *David wanted to impart to everyone his desire to bring the Ark of God to Jerusalem* so he proposed that they gather everyone to hear the vision. He said to them:

> *If it seems good to you, and if it is from the Lord our God, let us send everywhere to our kinsmen who remain in all the land of Israel, also to the priests and Levites who are with them in their cities with pasture lands, that they may meet with us* (1 Chronicles 13:1).

The agreement of core leadership is a powerful key in returning to God. The leaders agreed that all should come together (see 1 Chron. 13:1-4). David's vision was presented to the people and adopted by the nation. Thus, Israel developed **a shared vision** (Component #2) of bringing the Ark to Jerusalem.

The Ark of the Covenant had been crafted in the shadow of Mount Sinai according to God-given plans (see Exod. 25:1-22). The Tabernacle, and later the Temple, housed this magnificent creation. It was a wooden box lined inside and out with gold. Solid gold angels with wings spread stood on top, and the cover of the chest was a gold slab called the mercy seat. Jewish scholars estimate that the Ark weighed about 2,000 pounds.

Above the mercy seat, God's holy presence dwelt (see Exod. 25:22). Because God's sinless purity was manifest between the angels' wings, the Ark had to be covered before the Levites moved it, lest they touch it or see it (see Num. 4:15). But the Ark was not to be covered by any old sheet or blanket. Numbers 4:5 tells us that when the Ark was to be moved, Aaron and his sons (the priests) were to go into the Tabernacle and cover the Ark of the Testimony with "the veil of the screen." This means that whenever God's presence, in the form of the Ark, was seen by the people, it was covered in that beautiful veil. The New Testament reveals that the precious veil represented Christ's flesh (see Heb. 10:20). The Ark of the Covenant wrapped in the veil is a beautiful illustration of the truth that God was *in* Christ; the apostle Paul confirms this picture saying that, "*In Him* [Christ] *all the fullness of Deity dwells in bodily form*" (Col. 2:9). Paul later declared, "**God was in Christ** *reconciling the world to Himself*" (2 Cor. 5:19).

The people gathered (Component #4) and **obeyed** (Component #5) King David in a united effort to move the Ark. Israel assembled to bring up the Ark of God from Kiriath-jearim to Jerusalem (see 1 Chron. 13:5-6). It was a distance of only eight miles, but it would take longer than they expected.

They had started well on the road to revival: their leader was strong and godly; they had a powerful shared vision, and they were moving in obedience and unity. Their only error was that they had not gone to the Word to verify the plan for success. This mistake would prove deadly and would derail the revival for months.

We must be careful to do things God's way, rather than man's way, as we seek revival. Our way is almost always not God's way. The problem lay in David's choice of transportation for the Ark of the Covenant. David was ignorant of the prescribed method for moving the Ark. Apparently, everyone else was, too. Ignorance of God's Word can be dangerous, even if our motives are good. This incident also shows that even good leaders can make mistakes.

The Israelites put the Ark on a nice new oxcart. Attempting to carry God's presence on a manmade contrivance created a problem highlighted in the meaning of the names of Abinadab's sons, Ahio and Uzzah, who were guiding the cart. *Ahio* means "brotherly;" *Uzzah* means "to be strong." Being brotherly is good, and human strength is admirable, but human goodness and power will never usher in the presence of the Lord. Things went well for a while, but when they approached a rough spot in the road, the ox-drawn cart could not handle the bumps. There will always be some "bumps in the road" when you want to bring in the presence of the Lord. Uzzah tried to steady the Ark when it nearly fell, but human efforts to touch God and "hold the Ark," even when well-intentioned, will always end in disaster. God will not...cannot...allow sinful flesh to touch Him. Uzzah was struck down as a lesson to the nation. The only way we can approach God is when we are shielded from His awful holiness. David either didn't know or had forgotten this vital truth.

The results of ignoring God's plan were death, anger, and confusion. David became fearful and thought God had been unfair. He saw himself as having been rebuffed while trying to do something good. As a result, he blamed God. His ignorance of God's ways and God's holiness warped his view of God. David became unwilling to move the Ark of God. He took it aside to the house of Obed-edom (see 1 Chron. 13:7-13). When you don't understand events and blame God for the difficulties, you, too, will "park the Ark." God was simply acting in accordance with the demands created by His purity and our sinfulness. Like David, many draw back today when God strikes the flesh.

The presence of the Lord, however, brought blessings to Obed-edom's house (see 1 Chron. 7:14). For three months, good things happened to this man and his family. David heard of it and his desire for the presence of the Lord for Jerusalem was rekindled. He became spiritually jealous. May that happen to us—may we hear of God blessing and moving in other places and determine that we must have the Lord's manifest presence as well.

From David's youth, he had experienced the goodness of God. This led him to search the Scriptures for the answer to his desperate question: *How could a loving God strike down Uzzah?* Though distraught by the event, David didn't give up on God. This is a good lesson for us. When God acts in a way we do not understand, we must not throw up our hands in despair and walk away. We must remember the goodness of the Lord and turn to His Word to find the answer we need.

David had already prepared a place for the presence of God—a tent (see 1 Chron. 15:1). This is the Tabernacle of David mentioned in Acts 15:16, *"I will rebuild the tabernacle of David which has fallen, and I will rebuild its ruins, and I will restore it."* If we truly want the Lord's presence, we must prepare a place for Him and welcome Him. When the Ark finally arrived in Jerusalem, *that simple tent became a place of spiritual sacrifice, blessing, and continuous praise and worship.*

Apparently, the experience of temporarily housing the Ark made such an impact on Obed-edom that he became a gatekeeper at the Tabernacle of David (see 1 Chron. 15:24). Once we experience God's presence, we will never be satisfied away from Him.

They got direction from the Word of God (Component #3) and **consecrated themselves** (Component #14). During his search of the Scriptures David discovered that the Ark could only be moved by consecrated men (see Num. 4:15). Levites were selected and prepared for the task (see 1 Chron. 15:2,11-12).

The people praised the Lord (Component #6). When Israel followed God's directions, they were able to approach Him with confidence:

> *David spoke to the chiefs of the Levites to appoint their relatives the singers, with instruments of music, harps, lyres, loud-sounding cymbals, to raise sounds of joy. So it was David, with the elders of Israel and the captains over thousands, who went to bring up the ark of the covenant of the Lord from the house of Obed-edom with joy* (1 Chronicles 15:16,24-25).

STAGE TWO REVIVAL (GOD RETURNS TO HIS PEOPLE)

A miracle took place (Result #1). The wisdom of following God's plan was almost immediately apparent. When the Levites finally picked up the Ark and began to move it, they noticed something strange: it was not as heavy as they had expected it to be (see 1 Chron. 15:26a). If the Ark weighed 2,000 pounds and 12 Levites carried it, each man would have been required to support more than 150 pounds—a large weight to manage for any distance, even on your shoulder. They had walked only a few steps when it became obvious that God was helping the Levites carry the Ark. I love that God was helping the Levites! They immediately stopped and an additional **sacrifice** (Result #8) of seven bulls and seven rams was offered (see 1 Chron. 15:26b). Oh the joy that floods the heart of every preacher and worker when God helps the Levites!

The **praise and worship** really poured out then (Result #2), but this time it was a *result* of God's presence rather than a preparation for it. *"All Israel brought up the Ark of the Covenant of the Lord with shouting, and with the sound of the horn, with trumpets, with loud-sounding cymbals, with harps and lyres"* (1 Chron. 15:28). We are to praise the Lord at all times, but how wonderful and natural this becomes when He makes His presence obvious.

They had **great joy** (Result #3). David and (almost) all the people rejoiced as the Ark was brought to the city. David began to dance! Two Hebrew words are used to describe his actions. The first, *raqad,* means "to spring about (wildly or for joy)," while the second, *karar,* means "to dance (i.e., whirl)."[2] David laid aside kingly pride and his heavy robe so he could celebrate with everything in him—wearing only the simple linen ephod.

When the presence of the Lord is with you, you can rejoice in worship and not be bound by what others think. Praising and worshiping God with abandon is appropriate in the presence of the Lord. David's dance was especially sweet for him in light of the failure he had earlier experienced while trying to serve God in his own wisdom. But he pressed through to find complete victory. And he expressed that victory with his feet.

Opposition (Result #15) arises during these times of revival. And it often comes from an unexpected quarter. David's wife Michal gazed out of the palace window and saw her husband leaping, dancing, and celebrating with all his might. She judged his exuberance as totally unseemly and she "despised" him in her heart because of it (see 1 Chron. 15:29). It is sad that Michal disrespected David. She apparently felt embarrassed by his style of worship. The Word tells us that Michal actually loved David, but she did not have a love relationship with the Lord so it was impossible for her to understand David's joy. When David returned home to bless his household, Michal was scathing in her criticism, *"How the king of Israel distinguished himself today! He uncovered himself today in the eyes of his servants'* *maids as one of the foolish ones shamelessly uncovers himself!"* (2 Sam. 6:20). In response to her stinging accusation David replied,

> *It was before the Lord, who chose me above your father and above all his house, to appoint me ruler over the people of the Lord, over Israel; therefore I will celebrate before the Lord. I will be more lightly esteemed than this and will be humble in my own eyes, but with the maids of whom you have spoken, with them I will be distinguished* (2 Samuel 6:21-22).

Verse 23 tells us that, because of her critical attitude, Michal had no children to the day of her death. *Spiritual barrenness will always be the curse of those who despise true worshipers* and who fail to recognize the presence of the Lord.

REVIVAL THEME

David shows us the most important thing in any revival—that we must have the presence of the Lord. The corollary to this great truth is that we must learn that the only way we will have His sweet presence is according to His Word. David had a great desire to have the Ark of the Covenant in Jerusalem but all the preparation and excitement yielded only death and confusion until Israel discovered the correct way to move the presence of the Lord. So it is today, God will not be moved by fleshly conveyances.

ENDNOTES

1. A narrative based on Second Samuel 6 and First Chronicles 13 and 15.

2. James Strong, *Strong's Hebrew Lexicon*, 1890.

POINTS TO PONDER

1. David's desire to move the Ark of the Lord to Jerusalem was intense and correct. Why did he fail in his first attempt? What lessons does this teach us about our experiences in ministry?

2. There are three specific results from the aborted effort to move the Ark that the author points out. What are these consequences? Do they explain the attitude and atmosphere in some churches? If so, how?

3. When the Levites carrying the Ark had traveled a short distance, they reported a miraculous development. What was it, and how does it apply to ministry today?

4. Though Michal loved David, there was something about him she did not understand. What was this difference in their characters? How and why did this drive a wedge between them?

Chapter 5

THE SOLOMON REVIVAL
BUILDING A TEMPLE FOR THE LORD

THE FIRE AND THE GLORY[1]

David had been a giant. Though just a man, his passion for the Lord was so singular he would be held up as a prime example of a man after God's heart for generations to come. He reigned 40 years, forging a united kingdom by the force of his faith and will. Now one of David's sons sat on the throne. The transition of leadership had not been easy. Two other sons had each vied for the throne, but Absalom and Adonijah eventually lost their lives in an ungodly quest for power.

All that was past now; King Solomon had grown strong and consolidated power. As he stood in the court of the new Temple, he could still hear the words spoken to him by his father seven years before, *"Solomon, know the God of your father, and serve Him with a whole heart and a willing mind...for the Lord has chosen you to build a house for the sanctuary"* (1 Chron. 28:9-10).

The construction cost for the Temple had been enormous: praying, marshalling hundreds of thousands of workers, and expending vast treasure in order to follow the precious God-given plans his father had placed in his hands. Bending every effort to the huge task, Solomon had succeeded. Huge stone blocks had been quarried in the mountains. Giant cedar timbers had been floated down the coast from Lebanon.

After seven years of labor the magnificent Temple stood complete in Jerusalem. *Now the awesome building's pristine white limestone gleamed in the morning sun.* The structure had no equal on earth. At its entrance, two bronze pillars named Jachin and Boaz towered 60 feet high. Solomon gazed at them, recalling that the craftsmen had lost track of the actual weight of the huge castings. In the spacious court in front of the pillars, the laver sat astride 12 brass oxen. It held enough water to swim in. Every interior surface in the Temple was paneled in gold.

In the Holy of Holies stately cherubim bowed, their golden wings spanning the width of the room. Near the door of the court stood the altar of burnt offering; dark blood, just poured from sacrificial animals, was pooling at its foot. Wood was carefully stacked under the altar grate and the first of the sacrifices to be offered that morning lay prepared on top. Outside, the bleating of sheep and baying of oxen could be heard. This was dedication day.

Solomon surveyed the scene, satisfied that he and all Israel had done as much as humanly possible to prepare for that day. His eyes swept over the crowd. The elders of the nation were there, leaders of the 12 tribes standing together as brothers. Near the king were massed the singers and Levites. Cymbals, harps and over a hundred trumpets glinting in the morning sun were nervously handled by eager musicians. The priests stood ready, sanctified according to Levitical law. Tiny bells on the hems of their linen garments tinkled with every movement. All Israel was gathered expectantly in the wide court that stretched around the building.

The trumpets sounded and the singers led the assembly in praise and worship. Accompanied by the instruments, the people lifted their voices in song as one man to the Lord, *"Truly He is good, for His lovingkindness is everlasting"* (2 Chron. 5:13). As the singing swelled, priests carried the Ark of the Covenant into the Holy of Holies and set it in its permanent resting place between the massive golden angels.

As they exited the Temple, the House of the Lord filled with a cloud of glory! This supernatural fog spilled out into the court and sacrifices at the altar suddenly stopped. Solomon remembered Nathan's prophecy and breathed, *"The Lord has said that He would dwell in the thick cloud"* (2 Chron. 6:1).

When the cloud of glory cleared, Solomon stepped up to the small raised platform prepared for him near the altar. A hush lay over the crowd. The king raised his voice, strong and resonant in the great court, and blessed the people. He reminded them of who they were as a nation, of God's plan for them, and of His grace to them. Solomon then turned and faced the Temple, feeling his heart thundering in his chest. Spreading his hands in worship and submission, Solomon knelt and began to pray,

O Lord, the God of Israel, there is no god like You in heaven or on earth, keeping covenant and showing lovingkindness to Your servants who walk before You with all their heart. The highest heaven cannot contain You; how much less this house which I have built. Yet have regard to the prayer of Your servant and to his supplication, O Lord my God. Listen to the cry...of Your servant (2 Chronicles 6:14,18-19).

Solomon could feel the anointing upon him growing as he spoke. It was both sweet and overwhelming. His voice stumbled with emotion, *"Hear from heaven Your dwelling place, and forgive, for You alone know the hearts of the sons of men, that they may fear You, to walk in Your ways as long as they live in the land which You have given"* (2 Chron. 6:30-31).

He felt tears running down his cheeks. He had difficulty breathing, yet humble strength coursed into his words. *"Now therefore arise, O Lord God, to Your resting place, You and the Ark of Your might. Let Your priests, O Lord God, be clothed with salvation and let Your godly ones rejoice in what is good!"* (2 Chron. 6:41). Solomon began to tremble. The air was thick with expectation as he pleaded, *"O Lord God, do not turn away the face of Your anointed; remember Your lovingkindness to Your servant David"* (2 Chron. 6:42).

As Solomon's fervent prayer ended, the intense atmosphere seemed to explode. *Crackling with energy, intense light burst upon the altar as fire came down from Heaven.* Heat and sparks radiated everywhere. With consuming power, the blaze urgently devoured the wood, flesh, and bone on the brass altar. Smoke pillared above the city.

Solomon realized he was lying face down. Raising his head he saw the massive crowd also prostrate in worship. Moments passed in holy silence. Softly, at first from the singers, the familiar chorus was repeated, *"Truly He is good,* [for] *His lovingkindness is everlasting..."* (2 Chron. 7:3). Others joined in until all were singing. From where Solomon lay he could see through the open doors into the holy place. With wonder he watched the glory cloud roll out from between the cherubim and fill the Temple again. He turned his eyes downward and worshiped. No one had strength to rise, nor wanted to, for some time. Not until the next morning did the priests dare enter the Temple to replenish the golden lampstand and sprinkle finely ground incense on fresh coals brought from God's fire.

THE SETTING FOR REVIVAL

No one living that day at Solomon's Temple had ever seen God's presence manifest in fire, but it was not the first time flames fell from Heaven. Israel's history is marked with the Lord's appearances in fire:

- God appeared to Moses in a supernaturally burning bush (see Exod. 3:2).

- Mount Sinai was ablaze with glory when God met with Israel (see Exod. 24:17).

- One day fire consumed the offerings at the Tabernacle (see Lev. 9:23-24).

- The Angel of the Lord consumed Gideon's sacrifice by fire (see Judg. 6:21).

- Then came dedication day at the Temple.

- It was almost 400 years after the spectacular event at the Temple that someone else recorded seeing the fiery appearance of the Lord, as flames fell on Elijah's altar in the contest with Baal's prophets (see 1 Kings 18:38).

- Ezekiel described an awesome sight he saw coming toward him in one of his visions:

> On that which resembled a throne, high up, was a figure with the appearance of a man. Then I noticed from the appearance of His loins and upward something like glowing metal that looked like fire all around within it and from the appearance of His loins and downward I saw something like fire; and there was a radiance around Him"(Ezekiel 1:26-27).

In the New Testament, we also see the presence of the Lord characterized by fire. On the Day of Pentecost flames as of fire appeared over each of the 120 disciples in the Upper Room signifying God inhabiting and empowering the Church, His new temple (see Acts 2:3).

Our God *is* a consuming fire (see Heb. 12:29). The experience on dedication day at the Temple was an amazing, wonderful illustration of this truth. It was God "showing up." The Temple stood complete and magnificent, but empty, until the flames and glory cloud announced the presence of God in fiery acceptance and pleasure. The fire communicated boldly God's undeniable message: "I'm taking up residence!"

May the heavenly fire fall again. We need the fire of His presence in our day. A well-constructed building housing well-dressed people will never suffice. We need that holy incandescence. *We*, rather than Solomon's Temple, are the house of the Lord now. *We* are to be the place where He dwells in power! Israel had witnessed in awe the fire in earlier days; yet, it needed a consuming flame in Solomon's Temple. Similarly, the Church has seen God's glory in the past, but we need fresh fire today.

Some may question the inclusion in this book of Solomon as a revival king. After all, his father David was a great king, the prototype. But the last years of David's reign had been difficult ones. Prosperity and the passage of time had brought spiritual complacency and political challenges to the kingdom. Absalom, David's favorite son, was assassinated when he attempted to unseat his father in a military coup. Later, as David grew old and frail, another son, Adonijah, also schemed to replace his father. Contention ripped through Israel regarding who would be the next king—Adonijah or a still younger son, Solomon. David settled the issue by crowning Solomon as Israel's new king. Solomon came to the throne of a great kingdom, but one that was seriously divided, wounded, and confused. In the same way, even great churches can need revival after times of transition or conflict.

This revival was all about building the House of the Lord. God wanted a place where His glory could be seen and where the nations could meet with Him. In the fullness of New Testament revelation, we know that the Church is now His temple and the place where He is to be magnified (see 1 Cor. 3:16-17). The church God inhabits is not a building or earthly organization, but the "called out ones" who have left the world and are the dwelling place of the Most High.

STAGE ONE REVIVAL (GOD'S PEOPLE RETURN TO HIM)

A strong godly leader arose (Component #1). David knew that Solomon was God's choice to lead His people, *"Of all my sons...[God] has chosen my son Solomon to sit on the throne of the kingdom"* (1 Chron. 28:5). With the Lord's help, young Solomon quickly consolidated political power (see 2 Chron. 1:1). Then, we read of a critical development in Solomon's life and the history of Israel. Solomon, with the leaders of the nation, went to Gibeon, where the Tabernacle of Moses resided, and offered 1,000 burnt offerings (see 2 Chron. 1:6-7). God was pleased with this lavish expression of worship and appeared to Solomon that night. He made the young king a wonderful offer, *"Ask for whatever you want Me to give you."* Solomon responded, *"Give me now wisdom and knowledge, that I may go out and come in before this people, for who can rule this great people of Yours"* (2 Chron. 1:10). God was impressed with Solomon's humility; because Solomon did not ask for treasure and fame, God gave him wisdom...and included riches and honor as well. He became not only a strong leader, but a godly one. Solomon's later failings, while tragic, do not negate the fact that, at this time, he was the strong godly leader Israel needed.

Israel had a shared vision (Component #2). David imparted vision for building the Lord's House to Solomon—not only how to build it, but also how to administrate it (see 1 Chron. 28:9-13). Solomon obediently accepted his father's vision. Others *may* have the vision but the leader *must* have it, for he will have the task of imparting it to those who follow him. God-given vision must be accepted and embraced by the leader, his core advisers, and a critical mass of the congregation. After some initial confusion, **Israel followed Solomon as a united nation** (Component #5). Solomon models Christ's obedience to the Father as he fulfills David's vision while Israel illustrates the Church's obedience to Christ.

Most Christians understand that they must be obedient to the Lord; this is the highest level of obedience to authority. Where many struggle is in following and honoring *human* authority. How remarkable, or perhaps, how basic, that the Lord made a covenant with His people at Horeb *after* they assured Moses, *"Speak to us all that the Lord our God speaks to you, and we will hear and do it"* (Deut. 5:27). Despite their vow to obey God through Moses' instructions, rebellion against Moses' leadership was a constant problem.

It is undeniable that church leaders are fallible; tragically, they sometimes abuse their power. Nevertheless, Scripture directs us to obey them. For example, in Hebrews 13:17 we read *"Obey your leaders and submit to them, for they keep watch over your souls as those who will give an account. Let them do this with joy and not with grief, for this would be unprofitable for you."* Our safeguard against being led astray by human leaders is our knowledge of God's Word and our own relationship with the Lord. The writer of this key exhortation in Hebrews 13:17 appropriately adds in verse 18, *"Pray for us, for we are sure that we have a good conscience, desiring to conduct ourselves honorably in all things."*

Exercising good leadership is a great responsibility that needs powerful prayer support. Obeying leadership is also a great responsibility. The concept of obedience to godly human authority needs to be reestablished in the Church. If we are to have revival, God's people must come under authority and accept leadership. We must not only accept the Lord's direction on a personal level but understand that He leads and administrates through anointed individuals. It is the responsibility of every Christian to prayerfully accept a strong and godly leader. **Leaders and followers must be bound together with mutual love and respect.** No church or combination of churches will be able to accomplish significant ministry if proper attitudes do not exist toward leadership.

They received **direction from the Word of God** (Component #3). God told David concerning Solomon, *"I will establish his kingdom for-*

ever if he resolutely performs My commandments and My ordinances, as is done now" (1 Chron. 28:7). David then commanded Solomon,

> *So now, in the sight of all Israel, the assembly of the Lord, and in the hearing of our God, observe and seek after all the commandments of the Lord your God so that you may possess the good land and bequeath it to your sons after you forever* (1 Chron. 28:8).

Solomon had a good example to follow in his father; David's love for the Word was a great advantage to Solomon's emerging leadership. At the beginning of his reign, Solomon did order his ways according to the Word. We also know that he built the Temple according to the God-given plan. His obedience greatly blessed the nation. However, Solomon's later failure to follow God's Word led to disaster for generations to come.

Solomon gathered all of Israel on dedication day. It is recorded that all the commanders, judges, leaders, and heads of families and the whole assembly were there (see 2 Chron. 1:2). Something in this **unified gathering of the people** (Component #4) invites God's response. The same is true in other revivals. Psalm 133 tells us that the Lord commands a blessing where unity in Him is evident.

> *Behold, how good and how pleasant it is for brothers to dwell together in unity! It is like the precious oil upon the head, coming down upon the beard, even Aaron's beard, coming down upon the edge of his robes. It is like the dew of Hermon coming down upon the mountains of Zion; for there the Lord commanded the blessing—life forever.*

This is why the devil works so hard to promote gossip, rumors, and suspicion among brothers and sisters in the Lord; it is why he is so quick to point out the failings and "flesh" of other Christians and ministries. And it is why uniting pastors and members in shared vision is so difficult.

As he prepared to die, King David imparted the mantle of leadership to his son Solomon. He dedicated his immense fortune to the building of the Temple and, in almost the same breath, asked the whole assembly an important question: *"Who then is willing to consecrate himself this day to the Lord?"* (1 Chron. 29:5). The question was not, "How much will you give?" The question was instead, "Will you give *yourself* to the Lord? Will you set yourself apart to God and His work?" This is the actual meaning of the word *consecration*: "to be set apart." Sometimes, we think that it means being sinless; but *consecration* simply means "giving yourself to God." It can be seen that the leaders and **people did consecrate themselves** (Component #14) because verse 9 says that they offered willingly with a "whole heart" and that King David "rejoiced greatly." Consecration will lead us to give our time, talent, and treasure. Our King rejoices greatly when we give ourselves, and what we have, wholeheartedly to Him and His Church.

They gave to build the House of the Lord (Component #8). David publicly exhorted the people to help Solomon. He said, in effect, that it was God's work: in essence, David said, *I have given my all and this effort is worthy of your support.* David enumerated the stupendous amounts of accumulated wealth he gave to fund construction of the Temple. This is illustrative of the Father's provision for building the Church (see 1 Chron. 29:1-5). While the Temple was still only a vision, the people gave. They invested in agreement with what they believed. They willingly placed their treasure in God's hands and, still, they kept giving. In First Kings, we read that the gold given amounted to 108,000 talents. A talent of gold weighed 131 pounds. By present-day valuation, the gold alone was worth over eighty billion dollars, not to mention the silver, bronze, and cedar (see 1 Chron. 29:1-5).

They were willing to work (Component #12). Solomon assigned 70,000 men to carry loads, 80,000 men to quarry stone in the mountains, and 3,600 to supervise them (see 2 Chron. 2:2). Building the house of the

Lord was not an overnight process. It took an army of men working for seven years. The cost was enormous, not only financially, but also in terms of pain, time, and effort; yet, when the House of the Lord stood complete and the glory of the Lord swept in and fire fell on the altar, I imagine no one there questioned if the construction was worth the effort! Even now, we rejoice to see the Church grow. And one day when we stand on Heaven's shores, those who have labored for the Lord will have no regrets about their role in building up the temple of the Lord.

Solomon gathered the leaders (Component #18). Like his father before him, King Solomon summoned the leaders of Israel to Jerusalem. All the priests in the city **sanctified[2] themselves** (Component #14) (see 2 Chron. 5:11). Interestingly, consecration of the workers does not always occur as the first order of business. Sometimes this cleansing happens in stages as God's servants see His plan for revival unfolding.

The nation praised the Lord (Component #6). The Levitical singers, clothed in fine linen, and carrying cymbals, harps, and lyres, stood east of the altar. One hundred twenty priests with trumpets stood beside them. The singers were accompanied by the musicians as they sang, *"He indeed is good for His lovingkindness is everlasting."* God's goodness and love were recognized and He was praised for these qualities. This recognition of the nature and intent of the Lord is a powerful precursor, and a sweet benefit, of revival. They offered praise *before* they saw the holy cloud and fire. Many today want to wait until they see or feel something of the presence of the Lord.

The glory of the Lord filled the place (see 2 Chron. 5:12-14). This was the first manifestation of the glory cloud that day. It appeared again after the fire fell (see 2 Chron. 7:2). The result was the same both times. The priests could not stand to minister; no flesh can stand when God shows up in His awesome power and glory.

Solomon **prayed with *all* the assembly** (Component #7) of Israel (see 2 Chron. 6:12-42). Solomon's place of prayer was before the brazen altar of burnt offering. Everything starts at the altar of sacrifice. All effective prayer begins there. Solomon stood on a platform so he could be seen and heard by all in the court. He then knelt, with raised hands, and prayed a model prayer for all who seek revival: Solomon first praised the Lord. He said, *"There is no God like Thee, covenant-keeping, loving, and faithful"* (see 2 Chron. 6:14-15). He then referenced the Word, reminding God of His promise to David concerning the House of the Lord (see 2 Chron. 6:17). Finally, he appealed to the Lord's mercy, asking God to be merciful to Israel if they would repent and return to Him (see 2 Chron. 6:22,24, 26,28,32,34,36). He ended his prayer with three requests recorded in verses 40-42.

1. *"Hear our prayers now, therefore, arise, O Lord God, to thy resting place, Thou and the Ark of thy might!"* He was saying to God, "Please dwell in this place!"

2. *"Let the priests be clothed with salvation and rejoice in what is good."* In other words, "Let the leaders know you and do the right thing."

3. *"Do not turn away...remember thy lovingkindness."* In other words, "Don't reject us, but come to us out of Your love."

STAGE TWO REVIVAL (GOD RETURNS TO HIS PEOPLE)

A miracle occurred (Result #1). As Solomon finished his prayer, fire from Heaven ignited the wood on the altar. It is exciting to note what happened when the fire fell:

1. Sin was dealt with—the burnt offering, representing sin, was consumed (see 2 Chron. 7:1).

2. The glory cloud again filled the Temple.

3. **True worship poured forth** (Result #2). When they saw the fire and the glory, all the sons of Israel bowed down on the pavement with their faces to the ground.

- God's goodness and lovingkindness were again the focus. They said, *"Truly He is good, truly His lovingkindness is everlasting"* (2 Chron. 7:3). It must be noted, their response was neither lackadaisical nor halfhearted; it was, instead, wholehearted and fervent. There was no embarrassment in bowing down before the Lord.

- Worship is a response to the reality of God. When the fire fell, Israel knew beyond doubt that God was real. We should not think it strange to see people singing, proclaiming God's goodness, and bowing down before Him. These are reasonable things to do, because God is real. Fervent worship is right because God is real. It is not dumb; it is smart, because God is real. Abandoning pride and self in worship is not embarrassing. It is an honor, because God is *real*. It is sad when Christians gather and people do not enter into fervent worship. When we *spectate* instead of participate, in effect, we are denying the reality of God. Some might say, "Well, when I see the fire, then I'll bow down." The problem with that is the next time visible fire falls, it may be too late.

4. **Additional sacrifices were offered** (Result #7). King Solomon and the people offered a sacrifice of 22,000 oxen and 120,000 sheep. This offering was so massive it is difficult to imagine. Solomon needed more room for the animals, so he consecrated the middle of the court that was before the House of the Lord (see 2 Chron. 7:5).

5. **They observed the Passover** (Result #10). All Israel observed the feast. On the eighth day, they held a solemn assembly as required by the Law of Moses (see 2 Chron. 7:8-9).

6. **More people came in** (Result #4). A great assembly from all Israel gathered to celebrate Passover (see 2 Chron. 7:8). Growth is one of the treasured results of stage two revival. When we feast on the Lord, many will come. They will come when we, who know the Lord, return to Him and He dwells in us in fire and glory.

7. **They experienced great joy** (Result #3). Solomon sent the people to their tents, rejoicing and happy of heart because of the goodness that the Lord had shown to His people Israel (see 2 Chron. 7:10).

REVIVAL THEME

The Solomon revival is about building a place for the Lord's presence to dwell—not a magnificent building upon which no expense is spared but a magnificent people for which the highest price has been paid.

ENDNOTES

1. A narrative based on Second Chronicles 5-7 and First Kings 8.

2. The Hebrew word "sanctified" here is *qadash*. It is often translated "consecrated."

POINTS TO PONDER

1. Solomon accepted his father's vision to build the Temple. He also received provision from David. The Israelites then worked together for years to complete the Temple. How does this illustrate the New Testament revelation of our heavenly Father's desire for a people to dwell in; Jesus' declaration that He would build His Church; and our call to win and disciple the lost?

2. Why did God respond to Solomon's prayer with fire and glory?

3. The author poses the idea that the supernaturally lit fire on the altar at the Temple on dedication day represents some powerful truths for the Church today. What does it mean to have "fire" in the Church?

4. When the glory cloud filled the Temple the priests could not enter the House of the Lord. What are your thoughts about this?

Chapter 6

THE ASA REVIVAL
SEEKING THE LORD

SEEK THE LORD OR DIE![1]

A cool wind swirled the gray smoke of many campfires in the predawn light just beginning to reveal the looming mass of Jerusalem's walls. Groups of men were preparing breakfast, which, for the most part, consisted of cakes of dates eaten with bread baked on stones beside the open fires. For three days the men had been filtering into the area. Their tents now filled the Kidron Valley and dotted the Mount of Olives.

The gates of the city swung open at sunrise, their large timbers creaking. The men of Jerusalem began to stream out and join those that had assembled from all over Judah. A quick count showed there was a total of 300,000 men under arms. Most, of course, were not regular army; even so, this was a force to be reckoned with. As they prepared to break camp, there was a sense of optimism among Judah's forces that onlookers might have found surprising considering what the men knew awaited them the next day.

In the palace, King Asa rose from the floor of his chamber where he had been praying. He turned, crossed the room, and entered the door to the hall; two guards fell in behind him as he strode through the palace, buckling the leather breastplate of his armor as he went. He stepped into the soft morning light outside the palace and a ripple of movement crossed the ranks of the king's guard as they came to attention on the flagstone courtyard. The king was well-liked and respected by his men. Strong, astute, and a true spiritual leader, Asa had cleaned up the capital city, improved the defenses of Jerusalem, and built fortified cities throughout Judah. Consequently, the land had enjoyed peace for the first ten years of his reign. Now, for the first time, a huge threat loomed. Asa stepped up into his chariot, seized its brass rail, and greeted the driver. The chariot's matched bays snorted steam and stamped their feet waiting for the guard of 50 to lead the way to the East Gate.

Soon, the elements of the army camped nearest the beautiful gate noticed a flurry of activity. Trumpets sounded a salute and the king's guard marched out followed by Asa's chariot. The chariot and its escort did not stop until it had crossed the Kidron, passed the tombs of the prophets, and climbed the Mount of Olives to a clearing near the top. Pulling his cloak about him against the breeze, Asa stepped to the ground, briefly allowing himself to enjoy the view of the valley and city from his vantage point. The panoramic scene featured a breathtaking vista of the majestic Temple built by his great grandfather. Asa gazed at the city he loved and thought, *Lord God, how beautiful is your dwelling place.* Captains of thousands began to gather around the king; when the group was assembled, Asa passionately challenged them to defend the kingdom. His determination to take the battle to the invaders, combined with his confidence that the Lord would help them, infused those leaders with an infectious strength they would pass on to their men.

By the second hour of the day, the army was formed up along the road leading to Gaza. Asa gave the command to move out and again a trumpet sounded. The vanguard of several thousand led the way; a large standard emblazoned with a great lion flew proudly at their head. The king's chariot and guard came next. The rest of the army followed in companies; carrying large shields and long spears, they were an imposing sight. Judah's army was on its way to the valley of Zephathah, a 20-mile march, to join forces with the men of Benjamin before nightfall.

The sun was still high as Judah neared the meeting place. Alerted to their arrival by sentinels, the army of Benjamin, 280,000 strong, raised a shout at the sight of Judah's warriors cresting the ridge. Asa looked down on the encampment as his chariot negotiated the hill. The king knew Benjamin's men were renowned as valiant and able warriors. Asa smiled, but grimly thought, "Lord help us, they will need to be." The next morning would bring war with an imposing army almost twice the size of Judah's and Benjamin's forces combined.

The huge invading army lay camped to the north at Mareshah. Led by a shrewd and cruel general named Zerah, these invaders had come out of Ethiopia sweeping all before them and striking fear in all the kingdoms of the land.

After dinner, Asa gathered his generals to pray and plan for the coming battle. Later, as the stars started to sparkle in the night sky, the king toured the campground to encourage the men. He found them of good cheer; several companies of men were independently gathered in prayer. Songs could be heard rising to the Lord in different sections of camp. Returning to his tent with joy, Asa bowed down, lifted his hands, and said, "Thank You Lord, for teaching us to seek You." The king worshiped and prayed for some time before laying down to rest. Some of his attendants were surprised that he slept soundly through the night.

Dawn found Judah and Benjamin gathered around a rise in the valley of Zephathah where the king stood. Perimeter guards watched for the enemy's approach while the combined armies listened intently to the king. Asa simply lifted his hands to the heavens and called out, "*Lord, there is no one besides You to help in the battle between the powerful,*" gesturing to the north where the Ethiopian camp lay, "*and those who have no strength,*" indicating his own men gathered around him. "*So help us, O Lord our God, for we trust in You, and in Your name have come against this multitude. O Lord, You are our God; let not man prevail against You.*" The rumble of an "amen" rose from half a million men. As it died down, scouts announced the Ethiopians were assembled at the far end of the valley.

The two massive armies faced each other; both armies were confident, but for vastly different reasons. The Ethiopians had become accustomed to easy victories simply because of their overwhelming numbers. In sharp contrast, the men of Judah and Benjamin stood boldly in God's promise of protection. What could easily have been a long, drawn-out battle proved to be quick and decisive. Benjamin's archers began launching withering volleys downwind at the enemy formations. Again and again the flocks of arrows flew, leaving the bows with a rushing sound. Eerily accurate, those archers struck down multiple thousands of Zerah's men with a precision that staggered the African invaders. Judah's able captains then took advantage of the sudden consternation in the enemy ranks by leading a coordinated and ferocious ground attack. Despite their numerical advantage, the Ethiopians were unnerved by the determined onslaught of the Israelites and struggled to bring their superior numbers to bear.

From his vantage point on the ridge, Asa watched the battle unfold. At a crucial moment, as Judah and Benjamin were surrounded in a sea of opposition, Asa saw something like a shadow pass over the enemy's ranks. *Under the supernatural stroke of unseen majesty, the Ethiopians quailed* and the men of Judah and Benjamin scythed through the foe's columns.

Realizing they were somehow overmatched, the massive invading army turned and fled in terror. Judah and Benjamin pursued them as far as Gerar. Every soldier under the banner of the Lion of Judah knew that more than their bravery and skill was involved in the rout that developed.

Israel spent the next day gathering a huge amount of plunder, including sheep and camels. As the returning forces neared Jerusalem the following morning, the Spirit of God came on Azariah the son of Oded. He went out to meet Asa and the victorious army as they gathered again in the Kidron Valley. The prophet shouted, *"Listen to me."* As silence descended on the throng, he continued, *"The Lord is with you when you are with Him, and if you seek Him, He will let you find Him; but if you forsake Him, He will forsake you!"* Both the victorious army and the jubilant crowd that had spilled out of the city listened intently as Azariah again lifted his voice, *"For many days Israel was without the true God and without a teaching priest and without law. But in our distress we turned to the Lord God of Israel. We sought Him, and He let us find Him."* A cheer of spontaneous praise to the Lord rose from the people. Azariah turned to the king and said, *"Be strong and do not lose courage, for there is reward for your work."*

This word from one of God's prophets caused rejoicing, but it also sobered the crowd. They knew their victory was God-given and was firmly rooted in their return to the Lord. The prophet's reminder of how things used to be drove a resolve deep into their corporate consciousness that they would not return to the days of spiritual and political chaos and rebellion. Their sincere conviction to seek the Lord was further strengthened. Israel bowed and gave thanks to the Lord. Then they made a formal covenant that all would seek the Lord or be put to death!

THE SETTING FOR REVIVAL

Following the reign of Solomon, Israel struggled greatly. Though it was still a great kingdom, the nation was diseased at the core. The people's once clear devotion to the Lord was now clouded by idolatry and ignorance. King Solomon's death brought political turmoil and a struggle for control. The 12 tribes were deeply divided regarding who they would follow. Under a man named Jeroboam, the ten northern tribes seceded and soon fell into Baal worship. In less than 200 years the ten-tribe nation of Israel would be destroyed, never to rise again.

Led by Solomon's son Rehoboam, Judah and Benjamin also forsook the law of the Lord. As a result, God allowed Egypt to come up against them; even so, the southern kingdom did not repent. Rehoboam reigned for 17 troubled years. At his death, he was succeeded by his son, Abijah. Abijah half-heartedly tried to initiate some reforms, but failed in these attempts. He only reigned three years before he died. His son Asa acceded to the throne. King Asa came to power in a land whose leaders and people had turned away from God. The situation had deteriorated as society suffered the consequences of bad decisions; their nation was characterized by a lack of justice, frequent disturbances, and recurring war. The Bible says they even had divine opposition, *"God troubled them with every kind of distress because of their rebellion"* (2 Chron. 15:6). The good news was that, in their distress, the two-tribe kingdom of Judah turned back to the Lord. They sought Him, and He let them find Him (see 2 Chron. 15:4).

STAGE ONE REVIVAL (GOD'S PEOPLE RETURN TO HIM)

Under Asa's **strong godly leadership** (Component #1) Judah regained much of its power and glory. This revival was all about seeking the Lord. Asa's greatness as a leader was rooted in the fact that He was a God-seeker (see 2 Chron. 14:2). He led Israel back from the brink of disaster and again taught them to seek the Lord. Because Asa sought the Lord, those who followed him did likewise. Blessed is the church whose pastor seeks the Lord.

This lesson of the need to seek the Lord was so soundly learned that before this revival ended, Judah made a covenant that all must seek the Lord or die. We cannot force people to seek the Lord today. Coercion is not an effective strategy to win the heart. However, Judah's return to the Lord and their deliverance from disastrous circumstances illustrate the critical nature of what the Bible calls "seeking the Lord." The people of Judah knew that seeking the Lord was a good and necessary thing.

In Second Chronicles 14 and 15 *"seeking the Lord"* is referred to seven times. To *seek* means "to go in search or quest of, to try to find or discover by searching or questioning, to seek the solution to a problem, to try to obtain, to go to."[2] Seeking the Lord entails prayer and fasting, study of the Word, deep surrender, and worship. It is obvious that Israel developed **a shared vision** (Component #2) of drawing near to the Lord. All believers should have this passion for knowing the Lord intimately; sadly, many today are lackadaisical about seeking the Lord. Seeking the Lord is low on their priority list. They are too busy, unconcerned about revival, or simply going through the motions of living a Christian life without truly depending on God.

In Psalm 14:2 we read a troubling statement, *"The Lord has looked down from heaven upon the sons of men, to see if there are any who understand, who seek after God."* God is looking down to see people's hearts and behaviors. Will He find any who are seeking Him?

The unsaved and the carnal are looking for things other than God. Some are seeking to hold onto their lives; in Luke 17:33 Jesus warned, *"Whoever seeks to keep his life will lose it, and whoever loses his life will preserve it."* Many are content to seek the favor of men. Paul stated, *"If I were still trying to please men, I would not be a bond-servant of Christ"* (Gal. 1:10). Many seek only the fulfillment of their personal desires. Paul also lamented over those who had left him, and the work of the Lord, for other things, *"They all seek after their own interests, not those of Christ Jesus"* (Phil. 2:21). Others are money hungry, greedily looking for riches, not realizing *"the love of money is a root of all sorts of evil, and some by longing for it have wandered away from the faith, and pierced themselves with many* [a pang]*"*(1 Tim. 6:10). Some seek for signs rather than the Lord Himself. In Mark 8:12 we read that Jesus sighed *"deeply in His spirit,* [and] *said, 'Why does this generation seek for a sign? Truly I say to you, no sign will be given to this generation.'"*

As Judah sought the Lord, they realized that some things were not compatible with a life lived for the glory of the true God. Consequently, **they removed idols** (Component #15), doing away with foreign altars, spiritual high places, sacred pillars, and the perverse Asherim (see 2 Chron. 14:3). Many of these idols had been established during Solomon's rule. But the Israelites had added to the collection during the reigns of Rehoboam and Abijah.

King Asa essentially commanded Judah to do two things: seek the Lord and obey the Word (see 2 Chron. 14:4). The Israelites **demonstrated obedience** to Asa's commands (Component #5) by entering a time of **united prayer** (Component #7) and **honoring God's Word** (Component #3).

As Judah sought the Lord, they began to experience His blessings. The nation grew strong and prospered (see 2 Chron. 14:6). In the same way, we will find God's strength and blessings if we will seek the Lord. Scripture clearly teaches us that seeking the Lord will fortify our spirits:

> *He gives strength to the weary, and to him who lacks might He increases power. Though youths grow weary and tired, and vigorous young men stumble badly, and those who wait* [seek] *for the Lord will gain new strength; they will mount up with wings like*

eagles, they will run and not get tired, they will walk and not become weary (Isaiah 40:29-31).

Judah also enjoyed **peace** (Result 5). Asa said, *"We have sought Him, and He has given us rest on every side"* (2 Chron. 14:6-7). They knew the peace they were enjoying existed only because they were seeking the Lord. The New Testament guarantees us a supernatural peace and protection of the heart and mind if we seek the Lord:

> *Be anxious for nothing, but in everything by prayer and supplication with thanksgiving let your requests be made known to God* [seeking the Lord]. *And the peace of God, which surpasses all comprehension,* ***will guard your hearts and your minds*** *in Christ Jesus* (Philippians 4:6-7).

Judah continued to live and thrive in the Promised Land. Asa pointed out, *"The land is still ours, because* ***we have sought the Lord our God"*** (2 Chron. 14:6-7). The land had been given to Israel by God. It was a gift, just like our salvation. We must maintain our walk with the Lord to stay in an abundant and victorious life. The one who is seeking the Lord will stay in God's grace.

STAGE TWO REVIVAL (GOD RETURNS TO HIS PEOPLE)

Israel received **miraculous help** (Result #1) when **they were attacked** (Result #15). Judah and Benjamin enjoyed ten years of peace before Zerah the Ethiopian came against them with a huge army. The question is not *if* we will be attacked, but *when*. Some might ask why the Lord didn't stop the Ethiopian army before they got to Israel. After all, Asa and Israel were sincerely following God. The answer is that God sometimes allows the enemy to assail us, even when we *are* obedient, in order to demonstrate His power.

Asa did the right thing when opposition arose. He called on the Lord rather than man. Getting help from people is acceptable, but we must go to God first. Expecting help from humankind is risky business. Sometimes others *cannot* help. Sometimes others *will not* help. In contrast, God *can* help, and God *will* help if we seek Him. We actually offend the Lord when we do not turn to Him first.

Asa declared his complete dependence on God as Judah **prayed together** (Component #14). He said it was a battle between the powerful and those who have no strength; "The powerful" was Zerah with an army of 1,000,000 men and 300 chariots. Zerah represented the devil and his forces (see 2 Chron. 14:10-11). The ones who "have no strength" were Asa and the people of God. Asa had a combined army of 580,000 men— certainly nothing to sneeze at. Asa's army represents us in our natural abilities. But our strength, in the natural, is no match for the devil. Our strength against the devil lies not in our numbers, intelligence, talents, social status, etc. Rather, our strength lies in the Lord:

> *Some boast in chariots, and some in horses; but we will boast in the name of the Lord, our God. They* [the enemy] *have bowed down and fallen, but we have risen and stood upright. Save, O Lord; May the King answer us in the day we call* (Psalm 20:7-9).

God helped the Israelites when Zerah attacked; of course He did— many of the elements of the revival protocol were in place. The Lord routed the Ethiopians before Asa and Judah, and the invaders fled (see 2 Chron. 14:12). It was a huge victory that generated much wealth for Judah through the spoil they took from the Ethiopians.

God then encouraged Asa and the people through **prophetic ministry** (Component #14). Azariah's prophecy spurred Asa on. The king removed more idols from Judah and Benjamin and even from additional cities in Ephraim (see 2 Chron. 15:8). This illustrates something wonderful that happens when we seek the Lord—we are drawn to Him and away from the degradation and darkness of sin. Jesus said to His disciples, *"Keep watching and praying that you may not enter into temptation; the spirit is willing, but the flesh is weak"* (Matt. 26:41). The Lord exhorts us to pray, not that we will escape temptation, but that we might not fall when it comes.

Judah **offered sacrifices** (Result #8). Asa restored the altar of the Lord and Israel sacrificed to the Lord that day 700,000 oxen and 7,000 sheep from the spoil they had gained (see 2 Chron. 15:8). This extravagant offering is an example of the truth that the more we seek Him, the more we love Him; the more we love Him, the more we will give to Him.

A large number of **people gathered** to Asa (Result #4). Many defected to him from the ten northern tribes when they saw that the Lord was with him (see 2 Chron. 15:9-10). The northern tribes were Baal worshipers and often became enemies of Judah in open combat. As the power of the Lord flowed through Judah, others recognized the anointing and blessing that had come upon them. When we seek the Lord and obtain His favor, others will be drawn to us, even those who have opposed us. This is when mass numbers of people are saved as a result of revival.

The nation of Judah made **a covenant** to seek the Lord (Result #13). A desire and commitment arose in them to seek the Lord even more than they had been doing. The covenant was to seek the Lord God of their fathers *"with all their heart and soul"* (2 Chron. 15:12). They knew how much they had gained by seeking the Lord, so everyone was required to commit themselves to seek Him. This recently delivered nation agreed that whoever would not seek the Lord would be put to death, whether small or great, man or woman! It was a case of *seek the Lord or die!* This may sound extreme, but it illustrates the fact that we *must* seek the Lord. If we do not, spiritual death is the result.

The covenant-making was accompanied by **praise and worship** (Result #2) (see 2 Chron. 15:13-14). **Great joy** (Result #3) was evident as all Judah rejoiced concerning the oath (see 2 Chron. 15:15). When we have sought the Lord, and know His blessings, making a covenant to continue seeking Him is not an onerous task. The people were convinced it was a good thing to seek the Lord and acted upon this principle of life.

Still, more **idols were destroyed** (Result #12). Asa removed Maacah, his mother, from the position of queen mother because she had made an image to worship as an Asherah. Asa cut the idol down, crushed it and burned it at the brook Kidron (see 2 Chron. 15:16). When we begin to experience revival, we realize that even family practices and commitments must be rejected if they are in conflict with the Lord.

King Asa **gave to the House of the Lord** (Result #8). Asa brought into the House of God sacred things his father left him and sacred items of his own (see 2 Chron. 15:18). For some reason, the silver, gold, and sacred utensils were not where they belonged. Asa restored them to the Lord's House. When we return to the Lord, we are moved to give to the Lord what belongs to Him.

Peace (Result #5) came to the land again. The Lord gave them rest on every side and there was no more war for 25 years (see 2 Chron. 15:19).

REVIVAL THEME

All of the wonderful results in the Asa revival are directly traceable to the decision to "seek and obey." The importance of "seeking the Lord" and "obeying the Word" cannot be too strongly stressed. All of Scripture testifies to the power released in our lives when we do so. The world does not seek God, but the Church *must*. They do not know Him, but we do. If we are not motivated to seek for God and search for Him with all our hearts, let us return to the Scriptures, and read the clear message of Asa's revival again—*seek the Lord or die!*

ENDNOTES

1. A narrative based on Second Chronicles 14 and 15.

2. *Random House Unabridged Dictionary*, s.v. *seek*, Random House, Inc. 2006.

POINTS TO PONDER

1. Seeking the Lord entails determination, discipline, and desire, but the results are well worth the effort. What blessings did Judah receive as they sought the Lord under Asa's leadership?

2. The author states that seeking the Lord includes prayer and fasting, study of the Word, deep surrender, and worship. How would you describe what it means to seek the Lord?

3. Why do so few seek the Lord?

4. According to Second Chronicles 15:9, all of Judah, Benjamin, and a large number of people from other tribes joined with Asa. Why did these people come in?

5. Judah made a covenant that all must seek the Lord or be put to death. It was a case of "seek the Lord or die." How does this relate to us on a church level?

Chapter 7

THE JEHOSHAPHAT REVIVAL
THE POWER OF SANCTIFIED PRAISE

THE BATTLE BELONGS TO THE LORD[1]

A thousand men surged forward, overflowing the edges of the road. Behind them King Jehoshaphat led the combined might of Judah, but this advance "guard" carried no spears, shields, or swords. Rather, it was the corps of temple singers, dressed in linen, which led Judah into battle. They sang one of David's anthems as they marched; their voices rose in rich and powerful harmony, reverberating in the narrow valley they were passing through.

Among the thousand was a young Levite named Asaph. Fear assailed him as he thought about the enemy army awaiting them, but the song steadied his racing heart. It was one of his favorites; he lifted the stirring and reassuring words with the other men, "Give thanks to the Lord, His love endures forever…" *The majestic melody surrounded him and seemed to permeate his being.* Asaph sensed the Lord's presence in a way he had rarely felt. He looked around him; it was obvious that others felt God's power, too. He mused, "Well, if we are to perish before a sword we will fall praising the Lord!" As Asaph sang, faith rose in his heart: "Lord God, you destroyed the chariots of Egypt in the Red Sea and you struck down the walls of Jericho with a shout; You can give us victory today!"

The foe Asaph and the odd-looking army of Judah marched toward was a coalition of three armies—the Moabites and Ammonites, bitter foes of Israel, were joined by some of the Meunites, a desert tribe that lived south of Petra. The enemies had made no secret about their purpose to destroy Judah. They had advanced relentlessly toward Jerusalem from the east, skirting the Dead Sea, and climbing the wilderness slopes of the Judean desert.

King Jehoshaphat was shaken by the report of this advancing army. But, in his fear, he did the right thing; like Asa, his father, he set himself to prayer. He also proclaimed a fast throughout the land and the warriors of Judah gathered in Jerusalem at his call.

The previous night, thousands had stood in the court before the House of the Lord as Jehoshaphat led them in prayer: *"O Lord…are You not God in the heavens? And are You not ruler over all the kingdoms of the nations? Power and might are in Your hand….no one can stand against You"* (2 Chron. 20:6). Asaph was there, listening and praying with the rest, thankful for a king who loved the Lord. Though he was only 20, Asaph could clearly remember times when, at Jehoshaphat's command, idols had been cast down and crushed in the streets of Jerusalem. The king continued in fervent prayer,

Did You not, O our God, drive out the inhabitants of this land before Your people Israel and give it to the descendants of Abraham Your friend forever? [We] *have lived in the land and have built You a sanctuary for Your name* (2 Chronicles 20:7-8).

Jehoshaphat reminded the Lord of the promises given the people many years ago. God had warned that, *"should evil come upon"* (2 Chron. 20:9) Israel, they should, *"Stand before this house and before You and cry to You in our distress, and You will hear and deliver us"* (2 Chron. 20:9). "Amens" rose from the crowd as the nation sought the Lord. Jehoshaphat continued,

Now behold, the sons of Ammon, and Moab, and Mount Seir… are…coming to drive us out from Your possession which You have given us as an inheritance. [O God, help us.] *For we are powerless before this great multitude who are coming against us; nor do we know what to do, but our eyes are on You* (2 Chronicles 20:10-12).

Men, women, and children were there in the great court and surrounding area, many on their knees in fervent prayer. Asaph and most of the Levites around him were prostrate in worship. In the midst of the assembly, the

Spirit of the Lord came upon Jahaziel the son of Zechariah. He raised his booming voice in prophetic encouragement:

Listen, all Judah and the inhabitants of Jerusalem and King Jehoshaphat: thus says the Lord to you, "Do not fear or be dismayed because of this great multitude, for the battle is not yours but God's. You need not fight in this battle; station yourselves, stand and see the salvation of the Lord on your behalf" (2 Chronicles 20:15,17).

The words seemed to burn into Asaph's heart. Jahaziel continued, *"Do not fear or be dismayed; tomorrow go out to face them, for the Lord is with you."* The anointing was so powerful, the king and those still on their feet fell to the ground. Worship poured forth, at first in awe but then in joyful shouts of praise. Before long, the Levites spontaneously rose to their feet and began to shout praise to the Lord with all their might. They started to sing and the great assembly joined in thunderous praise to the Lord.

Asaph grinned as he walked along, "Yesterday was an amazing day...but today...we will write *new* songs about today!"

The air had been heavy with mist when the people gathered around the king at dawn outside the gates of the city. He said, *"Listen to me, O Judah and inhabitants of Jerusalem, put your trust in the Lord your God and you will be established. Put your trust in His prophets and succeed"* (2 Chron. 20:20). Asaph was standing among a large group of his fellow Levites. The king surveyed the crowd then made an announcement that stunned young Asaph…and his fellow temple singers, *"I propose that the singers and those who praise the Lord in holy attire go out in front of the army"* (see 2 Chron. 20:21). For a moment, Asaph thought he had misunderstood the king, but the murmur around him in the ranks of the Levitical singers confirmed that he had heard correctly. The *singers*, not Judah's proud warriors, would be the lead element in taking the battle to the enemy. The murmuring was not grumbling or rebellion, only initial surprise. To their credit, the Levites responded in faith and quickly agreed to lead the army. The mighty choir assembled at the head of Judah's army and, as the morning sun began to burn away the mist, the procession began to march to war.

On the valley road, the Levites now shifted to a powerful psalm of praise, and many of them began leaping before the Lord as they went along. Asaph felt the presence of God tingling through him. They were moving steadily toward the end of the valley where it emptied out into a dry wash leading down to the Dead Sea. The prophet had said the enemy armies would be there. Asaph's eyes swept the land ahead for any signs of them, realizing he was no longer afraid.

The Levites burst out of the valley and came to the barren edge of the wilderness. The amazing scene that greeted them brought their singing to a halt, not out of dismay, but out of shock. The attackers had reached this point but had come no farther. Corpses littered the ground by the thousands. Strewn over the desolate area were bodies and supplies in disarray. It was obvious a vicious battle had just taken place but not a single Israelite had struck a blow.

The amazed army pushed forward around the singers to view the scene of devastation. Asaph, suddenly in tears, found himself shouting, "The Lord, He is faithful! The Lord, He is faithful!" Others joined in grateful praise. Jehoshaphat directed scouts to advance; the few survivors they were able to find related that early in the morning dissension had arisen in their camp. The sons of Ammon and Moab had attacked the Meunites, wiping them out; and when they finished with them, they began to fight among themselves. In addition to their own violent attacks on each other, they reported that some awful unseen force had swept through their ranks striking men down.

After gathering the spoil, all Judah assembled in the valley. Jehoshaphat named it "Beracah"—the valley of blessing. He then voiced what they all knew to be true, "As we praised the Lord, He set ambushes against our foes. He has given us the victory!" The men of Judah then marched back to Jerusalem with great joy, Jehoshaphat at their head. Asaph and the rest of the singers led them in praise again, not to battle, but to the House of the Lord.

THE SETTING FOR REVIVAL

Jehoshaphat's father was King Asa, under whom Judah experienced revival. In some ways Jehoshaphat's reign was a continuation of Asa's revival. It is always a good thing for the kingdom when godly leaders succeed one another. However, we read that toward the end of his reign King

Asa stumbled badly. When Judah was attacked by the northern kingdom of Israel, Asa responded by bribing the king of Aram to attack Israel. The plan worked and Judah was spared, but Asa was then confronted by the prophet Hanani, who said to him:

> Because you have relied on the king of Aram and have not relied on the Lord your God, therefore the army of the king of Aram has escaped out of your hand. . . . the eyes of the Lord move to and fro throughout the earth that He may strongly support those whose heart is completely His. You have acted foolishly in this. Indeed, from now on you will surely have wars (2 Chronicles 16:7,9).

Asa was enraged at the prophet and unjustly threw him in prison. Later, King Asa contracted a disease that severely affected his feet. He did not seek the Lord first, but relied on physicians (see 2 Chron. 16:6-12). Because of Asa's spiritual struggles in his later years, spiritual confusion arose in Judah and the people fell back into idolatry. It was then that Jehoshaphat inherited the throne of the troubled kingdom.

When we mention Jehoshaphat, we immediately think of the worship team being sent out first in battle and the miraculous victory that ensued. But we will gain important insights if we examine closely what led up to the stunning triumph.

STAGE ONE REVIVAL (GOD'S PEOPLE RETURN TO HIM)

A strong godly leader arose (Component #1). Jehoshaphat strengthened his rule over Judah. He followed the example of King David and sought the God of Israel. The Lord was with Jehoshaphat and blessed him because of his obedience. God gave this king authority, riches, and honor (see 2 Chron. 17:1-4). The dread of the Lord was on all the kingdoms around Judah. Some of the Philistines and Arabians even brought large gifts as tribute to Jehoshaphat as he grew stronger and stronger.

Valiant men of Judah gathered around him and he was able to establish a large army (see 2 Chron. 17:10-19).

Judah returned to the Word (Component #3). The record says that Jehoshaphat followed the Lord's commandments (see 2 Chron. 17:6). All the kings of Israel should have done so; Moses had left instructions for all new monarchs:

> When he [the king] *sits on the throne of his kingdom, he shall write for himself a copy of this law on a scroll in the presence of the Levitical priests. It shall be with him and he shall read it all the days of his life that he may learn to fear the Lord his God* (Deuteronomy 17:18-19).

In response to God's Word, Jehoshaphat removed the high places and the Asherim from Judah (see 2 Chron. 17:6), **cleansing the land of idols** (Component #15). This was actually the second time he removed such idols. Someone was rebuilding the high places, but Jehoshaphat was determined these centers of religious idolatry would not stand. He realized the people needed to know the **Word of God** in order to change their ways, so he also established a nationwide **teaching ministry** (Components #3 and #20). *Teams of Levites and priests went regularly to all the cities of Judah to teach the Word of God* (see 2 Chron. 17:7-9).

Then Jehoshaphat made a huge mistake that almost cost him his life (see 2 Chron. 18). He allied himself with the ungodly Ahab of Israel in a war against Ramoth-gilead. It may have been his desire for unity between Judah and Israel that led to this unwise decision. Later in his reign, Jehoshaphat also partnered with Ahaziah, Ahab's son, thus repeating the mistake. Unity *is* critically important, but seeking unity with the kingdom of darkness is always a foolhardy quest. Jehoshaphat was almost killed in the battle with Ramoth-gilead. Upon his safe return to Jerusalem, the prophet Jehu rebuked him:

Should you help the wicked and love those who hate the Lord and
so bring wrath on yourself from the Lord? But there is some good
in you, for you have removed the Asheroth from the land and you
have set your heart to seek God (2 Chronicles 19:1-3).

God was not pleased with Jehoshaphat's error in judgment, but He knew the king's heart. This thought should encourage all who are longing for revival; for we have all made mistakes and exercised faulty judgment.

Jehoshaphat's close escape and the display of God's mercy profoundly affected him and resulted in immediate change in him and in Judah. He forged on in renewal and rallied the people from a wider region to the Lord (see 2 Chron. 19:1-3). Jehoshaphat appointed judges in the cities of Judah and exhorted them:

Consider what you are doing, for you do not judge for man but
for the Lord.... Now then let the fear of the Lord be upon you; be
very careful what you do, for the Lord our God will have no part
in unrighteousness or partiality or the taking of a bribe....Act
resolutely, and the Lord [will] *be with the upright* (2 Chronicles 19:6-7,11).

Then came the **opposition** (Result #15) that always seems to follow a return to the Lord. The combined armies of Moab, Ammon, and some of the Meunites came to make war (see 2 Chron. 20:1-2). Jehoshaphat was afraid and turned his attention to seek the Lord. He proclaimed a fast throughout all Judah (Component #17).

Little is said about fasting today, yet there are 74 references to fasting in the Bible. The Old Covenant required one day of fasting every year—the Day of Atonement. But godly men and women of both the Old and New Testaments sought the Lord in this powerful discipline. Elijah, Moses, John the Baptist, Esther, Daniel, Ezra, David, Hannah, Jeremiah,

Joel, Nehemiah, Anna, Jesus and the New Testament church all fasted. History consistently tells us that champions for God fast regularly.

The discipline of fasting must become a part of our walk and warfare. Fasting is a voluntary missing of food and drink (some include rest, pleasure, or other things). It is not starvation, nor simply dieting. Fasting must be coupled with spiritual desire expressed through the twin disciplines of prayer and Bible reading. Fasting is a way of declaring to God, "You are more important to me than life." Fasting is not a way of twisting God's arm, but of humbling ourselves, and drawing close to Him.

Fasting is powerful because man's enjoyment of the sensory world is an avenue through which sin attacks. Uncontrolled fleshly appetite felled Adam, Eve, Esau, and many others. Gluttony is a common problem today. Satan even tempted Jesus in the wilderness with food. Fasting helps us break the dominion of the appetites of our flesh. Rather than the flesh ruling us, we must rule the flesh.

Fasting cries out that spiritual life is more important than physical life. It shows that food is not the most basic essential in physical life; air is first, then water, then sleep, *then* food. Jesus set the example in this by fasting 40 days and 40 nights (see Matt. 4:2). He instructed us in how to fast and strongly implied that fasting is expected:

> *And whenever* [not if] *you fast, do not put on a gloomy face as the hypocrites do, for they neglect their appearance in order to be seen fasting by men. Truly I say to you, they have their reward in full. But you, when you fast, anoint your head, and wash your face so that you may not be seen fasting by men, but by your Father, who is in secret; and your Father who sees in secret will repay you* (Matthew 6:16-18).

Jesus actually proclaimed that we would fast. The disciples of John the Baptist asked Jesus:

> *Why do we and the Pharisees fast, but Your disciples do not fast?"*
> *...Jesus said...,"The attendants of the bridegroom cannot mourn*
> *as long as the bridegroom is with them, can they? But the days*
> *will come when the bridegroom is taken away from them, and*
> ***then they will fast*** (Matthew 9:14-15).

The early church fasted. The Book of Acts records this testimony from the first century church in Antioch:

> *While they were ministering to the Lord and **fasting**, the Holy*
> *Spirit said, 'Set apart for Me Barnabas and Saul for the work to*
> *which I have called them.' Then, when they **fasted** and prayed*
> *and laid their hands on them, they sent them away* (Acts
> 13:2-3).

Our attitude toward fasting should be positive. Too many people dismiss fasting out of hand or simply feel they cannot do it. We should be able to say, "It is God's will for me to fast." Those with physical concerns should consult their doctor, but Scripture reveals that we don't need a special feeling to fast and that fasting is not impossible. Temporary discomfort normally accompanies fasting, but our relationship with the Lord can profit immeasurably from this biblical discipline.

Many spiritual and physical blessings are associated with fasting. It rests and cleans our physical system. Fasting sharpens our thoughts and mental focus. Coupled with prayer and Bible reading, fasting builds devotion, faith in God, and discipline. The scriptural record reveals that fasting helped bring the following: deliverance from judgment, divine guidance and revelation, victory over fear, and protection in times of crisis.

Judah **gathered in unity** (Components #4) to **seek help from the Lord** (Component #5). Jehoshaphat stood before the assembly and glorified God, acknowledging His power. The king rehearsed the promises of God from Solomon's day. All Judah stood there united, including women, infants, and children (see 2 Chron. 20:3-13). *Together* they appealed to God about the threat facing them, and *together* proclaimed their dependence on Him. The power of calling on the name of the Lord in unity can not be overemphasized.

God encouraged them through **a prophetic word** (Component #16). In the midst of the assembly, the Spirit of the Lord came upon Jahaziel, a Levite. Through Jahaziel, the Lord gave them direction (see 2 Chron. 20:14-17). The prophetic word was that *God* would defeat the foe. Judah was required to do something however—they were to trust in the Lord and, "go down against them." In other words, God required them to act in faith—to go out to face their enemy. If they would do so, God promised He would give them victory.

The prophetic promise inspired faith and **worship** (Component #6). Jehoshaphat bowed his head with his face to the ground and the whole gathering fell down before the Lord in worship (see 2 Chron. 20:18-19).

With Jehoshaphat's wise guidance, Judah formulated **a shared vision in unity** (Component #2). After consulting with the people, Jehoshaphat appointed those who sang to the Lord and praised Him in holy attire to go out before the army (see 2 Chron. 20:21). This was a display of **obedience** (Component #4) and trust in the Lord. God had promised they would not have to fight, so they took Him at His word. The result was the most unusual battle strategy ever recorded…and one of the most amazing victories.

STAGE TWO REVIVAL (GOD RETURNS TO HIS PEOPLE)

A miraculous victory occurred (Result #1). When Judah began praising the Lord on their way to the battle, God set ambushes against the enemy. The enemy armies began to fight among themselves. The Ammonites and Moabites rose up against the Meunites and destroyed them completely and then began to fight against one another (see 2 Chron. 20:22-23). By the time the singers, Jehoshaphat, and Judah's army arrived at the battlefield, the victory was already won. After collecting the spoil, the people of Judah assembled in the valley. They blessed the Lord and called that place *"The Valley of Beracah* [blessing]" (2 Chron. 20:26). With Jehoshaphat at their head, the victorious army **joyfully** (Result #3) returned to Jerusalem, offering **praise and worship** (Result #2) to the Lord as they went (see 2 Chron. 20:27-28). The wonderful result of **peace** (Result #5) also came to the kingdom of Judah.

> *The dread of God was on all the kingdoms of the lands when they heard that the Lord had fought against the enemies of Israel. So the kingdom of Jehoshaphat was at peace for God gave him rest on all sides* (2 Chronicles 20:29-30).

Unfortunately the revival was limited in its length and scope. Second Chronicles 20:33 says, "The people had not yet directed their hearts to the God of their fathers." Without their strong godly leader they faltered.

REVIVAL THEME

Jehoshaphat and his brave Levites show us that when we are living in obedience to God, we can march forward with bold praise to the Lord on our lips, knowing that there is an unseen hand sending confusion to the enemy's camp.

ENDNOTE

1.   A narrative based on Second Chronicles 20.

POINTS TO PONDER

1. Jehoshaphat sought the God of Israel. He had learned from his father, who was a God-seeker. How can we pass on this trait of God-seeking to others?

2. Jehoshaphat allied himself with the ungodly Ahab and was almost killed in a war. He returned safely to Jerusalem, but the near-death experience and God's mercy profoundly affected him. Have you had a similar experience of God's mercy? If so, explain.

3. The Jehoshaphat revival features the discipline of fasting. What should our motive be in fasting?

4. When Judah began singing and praising on their way to the battle, the Lord set ambushes against their enemies. Do you make a practice of singing and praising the Lord when battles come? If not, why not?

Chapter 8

The Joash Revival
The Battle for Control

Bring Out the True King[1]

The glittering eyes of Mattan, priest of Baal, swept back and forth as he stalked the palace hallway. He'd lost count, but he made his way into what he believed was the last of the bedrooms. The young prince sleeping before him was only eight years old, but the man mercilessly extended his sword and slashed it across the boy's throat. Satisfied that the gory task of executing the princes of David's house was finished, he wiped the blade on the boy's bedclothes, sheathed it, and headed for the reception hall. Unseen by the assassin, in the deep darkness cloaking Jerusalem, two figures climbed out of a palace window and ran to the courts of the Lord's House. One carried a bundle wrapped against the night chill.

Though it was late, Mattan found Athaliah, the queen mother, still seated in the large hall impatiently waiting for him. He bowed and responded to her questioning look with a nod. Not satisfied, she asked in a brittle voice, "They're all dead?" "Yes." He replied harshly, yet with a slight bow, "All of them. The kingdom shall be yours, and Baal will be exalted." A twisted smile crossed her face as she rose, turned with an imperious swirl, and walked to her own chambers. When morning dawned, Athaliah, the daughter of Ahab and Jezebel, claimed Judah's throne.

A week later, Jehoiada, the high priest in the House of the Lord, entered the Temple a little before dusk. The tears in his eyes were threatening to overflow, even as he softly hummed a worship song. Other priests noticed that anger, grief, and shock were still close to the surface in this burly, but gentle, man of God. Jehoiada filled a brass bowl with coals from the altar in the courtyard, took the knife for trimming the wicks, the pitcher of fine olive oil, and the little golden bowl of finely ground incense and stepped behind the screen into the holy place. It wasn't his turn to care for the lampstand and burn the incense. But today he wanted— needed—to be in the presence of the Lord, and he knew the others understood. As he worked, he thought again, "How could Athaliah have killed her own grandchildren?" The evil act still staggered him. Coupled with the disaster in Samaria, it meant the line of David had been virtually wiped out in one awful week. King Ahaziah had insisted on leading his warriors into battle in Samaria. He and all the princes who went with him had perished there. With them gone, Athaliah had seized control of Judah by slaying the remaining males of royal blood.

Jehoiada agonized out loud as he worked, "The situation is disastrous, Lord, and it would have been hopeless if not for my dear wife Jehoshabeath." Jehoiada's wife had managed to hide one infant prince and his nurse; the three of them escaped the palace that awful night. The priest's clenched jaw relaxed a bit as he knelt at the golden altar. He slid the fresh coals onto their place and sprinkled incense on them. The sweet cinnamon tang of the special incense immediately wafted up and began to season the air. Jehoiada reached out to touch the horn on the corner of the altar. He spent several minutes on his knees there as he poured out his tears and his heart to the Lord. Once again, Jehoiada vowed quietly but passionately, "In your name, O Lord God, Athaliah's foul deed will not stand!" He rose and turned, running a strong hand along the edge of the table of showbread. The high priest would not linger in the Temple too long. He knew that Athaliah didn't dare enter the Temple grounds, but he had to make sure the baby stayed safe. That six-month-old baby boy was the only living heir to David's throne.

Jehoiada made his way to the storerooms in the Temple compound, where they had created a makeshift apartment. There, Jehoshabeath was preparing dinner and Rebecca was nursing little Joash. This infant would be king some day if Jehoiada had anything to say about it. Only a handful of faithful people knew who the little boy was who now shared the living quarters in the House of the Lord. Jehoiada hugged his wife and said to her, "If they had found you that night, I don't know what I would have done." Jehoshabeath smiled up at her husband with simple faith, "The Lord was watching over us."

For the next six years, Jehoiada and Jehoshabeath raised Joash in the Temple enclave as Athaliah led the nation deeper into Baal worship and depravity. When Joash turned seven, Jehoiada decided he could wait no longer. He called together five of his most trusted priests. The small band of earnest men entered into a covenant to bring down Athaliah and to crown Joash as king of Judah. Their plan was simple, but was fraught with peril; if Athaliah should discover their intent before they were ready, certain death awaited them. Jehoiada and the small group of conspirators sent a message to the priests and Levites they believed were still faithful to the Lord—all were to gather in Jerusalem at an appointed date.

Within a week, somber-faced men sat crowded in the high priest's house. Dispensing with pleasantries, Jehoiada brought out Joash and announced, *"Behold, a son of David; he shall reign, as the Lord has spoken!"* Stunned at the revelation that an heir still lived, the priests and Levites gladly made covenant with the young king.

Jehoiada then proceeded to lay out the plan he had prayed over again and again, "This is what we'll do. One third of us shall be gatekeepers around the city, one third will deploy at the palace, one third at the Gate of the Foundation near the Temple. We must all be committed and take our places. When you hear the trumpets, gather the people in the courts of the Lord. Remember, we are responsible for the safety of the king. Protect him at all costs!"

On the appointed day, Jehoiada handed out spears and shields from the Temple armory. The men deployed to their designated places. Though the priests and Levites were deadly serious, excitement coursed through them as they took their stand. The days of Baal worship had been dark, but now the true king would take the throne. Seven-year-old Joash and the stern-faced high priest took their places by one of the great pillars before the Temple. Looking overwhelmed and nervous, the young king stood close to his large mentor. The crown, specially made for him, was placed on his brow and he held a scroll inscribed with passages from God's Word. When all was ready, Jehoiada poured oil on the boy's head and proclaimed him king. The men in the court shouted, *"Long live the king!"* The shout was picked up as a chant by the phalanxes of armed men. *"Long live the king! Long live the king!"* With courageous determination, the men's voices rippled over the Temple walls and filled the city. The people of Jerusalem began running down the streets toward the Temple. The tumult grew joyous as people learned that a descendant of David was still alive. As the court filled, a bevy of trumpeters sounded a salute to the new king. The song leader motioned to the musicians and singers and a hymn of praise rose to the Lord.

In the nearby palace, Athaliah heard the commotion and stormed into the court of the Temple. She saw the boy, crowned, flanked by armed men on both sides and realized what was transpiring. She would have been wise to retreat, but blinded to the danger by her desire for control, she tore her clothes and began to shout, "Treason! Treason!"

Jehoiada was ready to deal with her. Without hesitation, he issued an order of execution and firmly said, *"Bring her out!"* He added, "Put to death anyone who follows her." Four men seized Athaliah and led her, kicking and fighting, out of the Temple. When they reached the entrance of the Horse Gate, she struggled with surprising strength and broke free. But Elishaphat speedily caught her; grabbing her wrist, he spun her around. His drawn sword slipped between her ribs and through her heart. Blood ran from her lips in a cough and she slumped to the ground. Unceremoniously they dragged her lifeless body well outside the city.

The residents of Jerusalem gathered in the House of the Lord and made a covenant with God. They would once again be the Lord's people. Then, making their way to the temple of Baal, they smashed his images and destroyed the Canaanite shrine. Mattan, the murderous priest of Baal, died, crushed under tons of stone, as the pagan temple fell.

Led by the nobles and rulers, the people of Judah brought the young king to the palace and placed him on the throne of David. All Jerusalem rejoiced and celebrated that night as peace settled on the city. Wicked Athaliah was dead and the rightful heir sat on the throne of Judah.

THE SETTING FOR REVIVAL

The time was 800 years before the birth of Christ and the situation in Judah was tragic and appalling. Something had gone dreadfully wrong. The kingdom was struggling spiritually, locked in apathy and apostasy. Then, a series of events occurred that threatened God's very plan of salvation; the enemy schemed to destroy the promise of a savior born of David's seed. The royal line came under attack. King Azariah, a descendant of David, ruled in Judah, but this man was a wicked ruler. He and the other men of David's line, including some of the young princes, visited their fellow Baal-worshiper, King Ahab, in Samaria. This was a dangerous time; Ahab was at war with the Aramaens. The nobles of Judah were caught up in the conflict and all were slain (see 2 Chron. 22:8-9).

In Jerusalem, some children of David's line grieved the deaths of their fathers. But in this moment of political confusion and weakness in the kingdom, wickedness arose to take control. Athaliah, the evil daughter of Ahab and Jezebel, and mother of the slain king, ordered the execution of all the remaining offspring of David's house (see 2 Chron. 22:10). This was an act of unspeakable evil. Not only were they children, but among them were her grandsons.

This was a coup on both earthly and spiritual levels, for Athaliah craved not only personal power, but also wanted Judah to become a center for Baal worship. If Athaliah's plot had been entirely successful, it would have done incalculable damage, for salvation's promise was linked to David's descendants. Today, the enemy still schemes to steal, kill, and destroy. Godly authority is usurped by the rebellious and ungodly. Satan wars against God and the heirs of the Kingdom.

Satan had a bloodthirsty scheme, but God had a plan too! That grisly night at the palace, all would have been lost if not for the courage of a godly woman. Few people know her name, but she was a genuine heroine. When the children were being killed, Jehoshabeath, wife of the high priest, hid one infant. At the risk of her own life, she rescued him and his nurse. The little boy's name was Joash; through him the line of David was preserved. Jehoshabeath's husband, Jehoiada, is the second hero in this story. He was the high priest and a true servant of the Lord. For six years this godly couple hid the prince from Athaliah and raised him in the Temple. For six long years, the murderous Baal-worshiper Athaliah ruled and the land languished in her satanic grip. But God had Jehoshabeath and Jehoiada. In their hearts, beat a desperate longing for revival and in the House of the Lord dwelt the true king (see 2 Chron. 22:11-12).

STAGE ONE REVIVAL (GOD'S PEOPLE RETURN TO HIM)

In the seventh year of Athaliah's evil reign, Jehoiada *"strengthened himself"* (2 Chron. 23:1). The principle of **the strong godly leader** (Component #1) arising in a time of weakness and turmoil is seen again and again in the scriptural accounts of revival. The Joash revival is different from most of the others in that Jehoiada, the real force behind the revival, was not the king. But Jehoiada's heart was filled with wisdom and courage. He stood up for God and protected the young king. When the time was right, he rallied Judah to the side of Joash. Together, they brought down Athaliah and destroyed the temple of Baal.

Jehoiada mentored Joash for many years and helped him lead Judah into a powerful revival. As long as the high priest was alive, the revival continued. Thankfully, he lived to a ripe old age, but when he died, Joash and the people fell away from the Lord.

The Joash revival reveals the power of influence. Key godly leaders can arise and influence people and events even though they may not be the paramount leader. If their heart is right and they work in respectful concert with the acknowledged leader they can have great effect. In fact, it may be impossible to have wide-ranging revival without these individuals who support, counsel, and guide a more prominent leader.

Jehoiada **gathered a group of key leaders** (Component #18). He had five trusted men, just a handful, but they were captains of hundreds (see 2 Chron. 23:1). A lone voice is good, if need be, but strength is found when brothers band together. These leaders **made covenant** (Component #9) with each other, and so must we. Without covenant relationship, any movement to return to the Lord will be weak and easily stopped (see 2 Chron. 23:3). Their covenant was centered on the **common vision** (Component #2) of removing Athaliah and crowning Joash.

Next, they sought other leaders with whom to share the vision. Each of these others had to decide which side he would be on and with whom he would cast his lot. They could refuse to get involved, but that would be, in essence, supporting Athaliah. If they stood with Jehoiada and his band, they faced certain death if caught. When this larger group of leaders met, Jehoiada introduced them to seven-year-old Joash and challenged them, *"Behold the king's son shall reign!"* He was saying, "The kingdom is now held by Athaliah, but God's will is that the rightful king take his place on the throne." They also gladly made covenant with the young king (see 2 Chron. 23:3).

This moment of clarity and commitment is always a turning point. When leaders share a vision and determine to apply it, real progress toward revival will start to take place. The message of the revival protocol needs to be passed on to a growing band of leaders who will take action. We must share a common goal, a common vision, and a common commitment to defeat satan and enthrone Christ, the true King, in the hearts and lives of his people. Once we know the true heir lives, we must draw together and agree that *He* shall reign. It is true that the world lies in the grasp of evil. But God still has a designated heir who is to rule all. "Behold the king's son shall reign *as the Lord has spoken*." Let us reveal the hidden Prince. His name is not *Joash*, which means "the Lord is strong." His name is Jesus—the Lord is salvation. Who has the courage to say, "We will not let evil rule! Enough of Athaliah; here is the true king"? Church leaders must not be content with simply having the heir to the throne secretly dwell in our house, for He is to be King of all.

Israel returned to the Word (Component #3). Jehoiada appealed to the Word when proclaiming that Joash must rule, "…as the Lord has spoken." He then proposed a plan of action that the leaders accepted; by doing this, **they came under authority** (Component #5). This is a crucial step. Unfortunately, leaders often vie for power and position among themselves. Jehoiada's plan was a shrewd one, laced with military precision. Yet, someone could have objected to the timing or method. Thankfully, they recognized Jehoiada's authority and acted in unity and obedience.

The plan was a practical strategy for victory; it involved deploying in three groups, each with unique responsibilities. The rest of the people would gather in the courts of the Lord (see 2 Chron. 23:4-5). We also need practical strategies in our struggle with modern-day "Athaliahs"— those who strive to wrest control from godly authority. These strategies are about how we actually gather, take our stand, and depose the enemy.

Jehoiada gave instructions concerning preparation: First, don't let anyone into the House of the Lord except the priests and ministering Levites. In other words, keep the House of the Lord holy. Second, prepare for war, be ready to fight; Jehoiada knew that Athaliah wouldn't give up easily. He equipped the men with spears and shields from the Temple. This illustrates the need of spiritual weapons. Finally, protect the king. The Levites protectively surrounded the king with weapons in hand. They were not to let the king out of their sight (see 2 Chron. 23:7). Everything depended on his survival.

Let me speak a word to those who are near strong godly leaders. There is a need for armor bearers for key individuals, because they will be attacked. Sometimes these key individuals underestimate their importance. It is easy for them to believe they are not necessary. After all, God is in control. It sounds humble for them to say, "Don't worry about me. Revival doesn't depend on me." The truth is that revival always depends on an alliance between God and man. The vision and passion of a strong godly leader *are* needed to forge this alliance. God could do it all by Himself, but He has chosen to work through people. If the devil can destroy, weaken, or wound key leaders, the work of the Kingdom will be set back. The church craving revival must protect the man of God.

An even larger group gathered in unity (Component #4). There was a sense of eager participation in a great cause. All the priests and Levites were involved, *"Jehoiada did not dismiss any of the divisions"* (2 Chron. 23:8,10). In other words, they all had their places in the plan and were expected to be present. We must be organized and committed like they were. Everyone should be involved and do their part. There must be no "divisions of Levites" dismissed or excluded from revival.

Praise was lifted to God (Component #6). The people of Jerusalem exalted Joash by crowning him king and giving him the covenant. They anointed him and said, *"Long live the king!"* Similarly, we must experience a coronation of Jesus in our hearts. We must *"give him the testimony"* and *"put the crown on him"* (2 Chron. 23:11). We must anoint Him with our praise. Revival will never happen if Jesus is not recognized and exalted as King in the House of the Lord. When spiritual leaders in Jerusalem exalted the new king, everyone heard and began to run to the Temple (see 2 Chron. 23:12). In the same way, exuberant heart-felt praise of Jesus attracts others. Lord, hasten the day when people run to the Church because we are praising you.

It is clear why the inhabitants of Jerusalem were joyful. After all, they thought all of David's descendants were dead. Reports of the surviving heir and his ascendancy to the throne were tremendous good news. They rejoiced to see the end of Athaliah's reign, for she had been a cruel tyrant. It reminds us of a joyful Sunday morning in Jerusalem 2,000 years ago when another Prince was found to be alive!

Opposition always follows revival (Result #15). All that commotion in the city attracted someone else's attention: Athaliah rushed to the Temple to see. And she was furious when she saw young Joash wearing a crown, captains and trumpeters at his side, and the people rejoicing and praising God (see 2 Chron. 23:12-13). Athaliah protested vociferously against crowning the true king. Like her mother Jezebel, she wanted to be in control. Similarly, the devil is never pleased when Jesus is given the proper place in our churches. The spirit of dead and false religion will always fight against revival. But Jehoiada was ready for her. He forcefully removed Athaliah from the House of the Lord and ordered her execution. We also must be ready to deal with the spirit of Athaliah. When she shows up, we must, with courageous determination, put her to death with the sword—the Word of God (2 Chron. 23:14-15,21).

More people (Component #4) came into the city. Those who had not been aware of the struggle to bring Joash to power now started to stream into Jerusalem. The covenant was broadened to include them. We, too, must welcome all who come to the King. This requires acceptance and love for all those who will arrive once the King is in place (see 2 Chron. 23:16).

Idols were destroyed (Component #12). Israel made it clear who they were going to follow—they were the Lord's people, not Baal's. They went to the house of Baal and tore it down. They broke its altars and slew its priest (see 2 Chron. 23:17). We, too, must tear down the spiritual pretenders to the throne and remove their influence from our lives and assemblies.

Ministry was set in order (Result #6). A system of spiritual authority was reestablished in the House of the Lord (see 2 Chron. 23:18-20). Often, ministry is weak and organization in God's House is poor because of the battle, and because of a lack of support. One of the wonderful results of revival is a strengthening and expansion of ministry.

STAGE TWO REVIVAL (GOD RETURNS TO HIS PEOPLE)

Great joy (Result #3) arose (see 2 Chron. 24:14). Similarly, if we apply the revival protocol we will bring out the King, present Him to the whole city, and all will rejoice in His presence.

Jerusalem finally quieted and **peace began to reign** (Result #5) (see 2 Chron. 24:14). Athaliah was dead; the struggle for control had been settled. The enemy was defeated, and the rightful king reigned over his city.

REVIVAL THEME

The story of Joash and his brave mentor, Jehoiada, reveals to us that revival always entails a struggle for control. The health, stability, and power of the Kingdom of God in local churches hang in the balance. We must be courageous and stand with the true King—Jesus, the rightful Ruler. He must be crowned in our midst and the spirit of false religion driven out of our presence.

ENDNOTE

1.   A narrative based on Second Chronicles 22 and 23.

POINTS TO PONDER

1. Athaliah seized control of the kingdom. Her goal was not just personal power but changing who and how Judah worshiped. What parallels can we see in the Church today in the struggle for control that is often evident?

2. The spirit of dead and false religion will always fight the true King and the revival He brings. How do the spirits of Athaliah and her mother Jezebel manifest themselves in the Church today?

3. Jehoiada and Jehoshabeath are not household names, but the kingdom of David was preserved through their bravery. Why was this critically important?

4. All would have been lost but for the courage of a godly couple who harbored the rightful king and brought him forth to confront Athaliah. This was dangerous but much was at stake. Have you joined those who stand with the true heir of David's throne?

Chapter 9

THE HEZEKIAH REVIVAL
CONSECRATION

SMASHING THE SNAKE[1]

H ezekiah walked up the stone steps and across the wide landing to the entrance of the Temple. The doors, fashioned of rich cypress and clad in gold, were deeply worked with figures of cherubim, palm trees, and flowers. The king's fingers slowly traced some of the carvings as he admired the craftsmanship noting, with satisfaction, that the repairs he had ordered done to the doors had been exquisitely well done. Hezekiah pushed lightly and the heavy panels swung easily on their pivots. Sunlight flooded in and gold glinted from the interior, but Hezekiah frowned as he saw some things he knew didn't belong in the holy place. The young king didn't enter but stepped back.

Twenty-five years old and still in the first year of his reign, reopening the House of the Lord was one of his first official acts. Hezekiah turned and looked at Isaiah;

the old prophet grimly nodded. Together they walked purposefully to the court on the east side of the great Temple. There, in the large stone-paved area, stood a gathering of priests and Levites. Upon the arrival of the king and the prophet, the burble of conversation subsided. For long moments, Hezekiah surveyed the men and the Temple compound. Scattered around the court were many pillars and shrines to the Lord and other gods; Hezekiah eyed one near the gate. Rather repelling in appearance, it was, nonetheless, a revered icon and symbol of God's mercy. It consisted of a rough timber extending vertically from a limestone base; at shoulder height another timber crossed it; draped on the cross member was a snake made of brass. The people called it Nehushtan, meaning "the great snake." It had been created at the Lord's direction almost 700 years earlier when the people, impatient in their wilderness journey, had accused God and Moses of plotting their demise. The Israelites complained and grumbled, even saying they "loathed" the bread that the Lord provided every day. God's anger was kindled; He sent poisonous serpents slithering among the tents. The vipers bit many and thousands died. The people realized their error, confessed their sin, and appealed for mercy; so God instructed that a brazen serpent be made and fitted on a wooden support. Anyone bitten would be healed if they would look to the symbol of sin lifted on a cross. Hurriedly, the strange figure had been fashioned. It proved to be the only deliverance from the poisonous venom. Though once used by God, the ancient relic had become a snare to Israel. The people came to worship the brass snake—even burning incense before it.

The king strode purposefully across the wide court, reaching the stark display; he took hold of the snake with both hands and lifted it off the cross piece on which it rested. He shuddered as he saw shiny places on the brass surface worn smooth by years of adoring touches and kisses. He turned to face curious eyes. Slowly, he raised the snake, its stone eyes sparkling in the sun. Suddenly, he swung it with all his might against the stone base. Quickly cast and not well tempered, *the snake shattered in shards that spun, scraping and skittering across the large flagstones.*

A moment of shock paralyzed the men before they shouted in outrage. If he had not been king, Hezekiah most certainly would have died that day. Respect for his office was one of three things that held the Levites back from rushing him. The second was Isaiah stepping to the side of the young king. The third was the look on Hezekiah's face. With eyes unafraid, he withstood the crowd of men and began to speak, *"Our fathers have been unfaithful and have done evil in the sight of the Lord our God."* The men grudgingly quieted but continued to glare. They *"have forsaken Him and turned their faces away from the dwelling place of the Lord"* (2 Chron. 29:6). The words were simple, but powerful and now began to come with heated passion, *"They shut the doors of the porch and put out the lamps, and have not burned incense or offered burnt offerings in the holy place to the God of Israel"* (2 Chron. 29:6). Some of the men visibly flinched and put their heads down, but many eyes still flickered with anger. All listened with rapt attention as he continued, *"Therefore the wrath of the Lord has been against Judah. He has made us an object of terror, of horror and hissing, as you have seen with your own eyes"* (2 Chron. 29:6).

Hezekiah's voice broke, *"Our fathers have fallen by the sword, and our sons and our daughters and our wives are in captivity for this"* (2 Chron. 29:6). He gestured at the other idols in the court and the remains of Nehushtan.

Powered by the Holy Spirit, the truth cut through rationalizations and anger to the heart of these men who were sworn servants of the Lord. Conviction actually felled a few to their knees. Hezekiah paused, tears welling in his eyes. Behind him, the magnificent Temple stood in mute testimony. He had prayed about this moment; strength rose up in him again and his voice steadied. *"Listen to me, O Levites. Consecrate yourselves now!"* (2 Chron. 29:6). Raising his arms to encompass the Temple compound he cried out, *"Carry the uncleanness out from this holy place!"* (2 Chron. 29:6). The words struck the bearded men with almost physical power.

There are moments in time that change history. This was such a moment. Later Hezekiah wondered if some of the men gathered there had been waiting, wanting someone to call them to their task. With a surge, a number of Levites moved toward the king. They weren't coming to kill him, but to follow him: Mahath and Joel, Kish and Azariah, Joah and Eden, his son; Shimri and Jeiel; Asaph, Zechariah, and Mattaniah; Jehiel and Shimei; and from the sons of Jeduthun, Shemaiah and Uzziel. Hezekiah counted 15—not as many as he had hoped, but he noted they were some of the strongest and most influential of the men. He could see tears on their faces. They gathered to him at the foot of the stairs before the great pillars. The king extended his hands to them and together they made covenant.

Eight days later the group sharing a vision to cleanse the House of the Lord had grown—their ceremonial consecration complete, dozens of priests began carrying items from the inner recesses of the Temple. Their demeanor was serious, but the king saw a joy among them as they went about their work. As they emerged from the Temple they were met at the doors by a stream of Levites who transported the items through the Dung Gate on the south side of the city and threw them on the dump in the Valley of Hinnom. The job was daunting; an accumulation of generations of personal items and trash had to be removed from storerooms. Asherim and stone pillars erected to other gods had to be smashed and carried out. The pieces of Nehushtan were swept up and melted down. So began the greatest revival ever witnessed in Judah.

THE SETTING FOR REVIVAL

Ahaz, Hezekiah's father, was an evil king who turned Judah away from the Lord. He served false gods, even sacrificing some of his own children by fire. Slavery and war marked his reign and the worship of Baal and other gods proliferated. The Temple was closed and the priesthood inactive (see 2 Chron. 28:19,22). The kingdom slipped deeply into economic and spiritual poverty, and it seemed apparent that the nation would fall to Assyria.

STAGE ONE REVIVAL (GOD'S PEOPLE RETURN TO HIM)

What a time to inherit the throne. History would not have blamed Hezekiah if he had given up, but the young man was not a quitter. Instead, he arose as **a strong godly leader** (Component #1) who did right in the sight of the Lord (see 2 Chron. 29:1). Such were his passion and commitment to follow the Lord that Second Kings 18:5 states that there were "none like him among all the kings of Judah, or any that were before him." Hezekiah's name means: "whom Jehovah has strengthened." Individuals must be strengthened by the Lord to lead well, for even fine intelligence, character, and personality will not suffice by themselves. With divine strength, Hezekiah brought Judah back from the brink of destruction. If revival is to come, we must have some who will rise up like Hezekiah did. When handed a situation in turmoil, someone must find a supernatural strength in the Lord to lead.

Hezekiah's example teaches us that, though it will not be accepted by all, strong godly leaders must bring a challenge to God's people to consecrate themselves and cleanse the House of the Lord. There are some who serve in ministry who long for someone to arise and call them to return wholeheartedly to the Lord.

Hezekiah began his reign by demonstrating **a concern for the House of the Lord** (Component #11). He opened the Temple, which had fallen into disuse (see 2 Chron. 29:3). He also authorized repair of the doors which had been stripped of their gold cladding to pay tribute to a stronger kingdom.

Under Hezekiah's leadership **a shared vision** (Component #2) developed. Hezekiah's revival was all about creating a foundation for societal transformation by cleansing the House of the Lord and consecrating the priesthood. This was necessary because what had started as neglect of the Temple in the administration of Hezekiah's grandfather had become nationwide spiritual revolt against God. Hezekiah's father had despised the Temple, and now Judah was near collapse. Hezekiah understood that Judah was reaping the consequences of separating themselves from the Holy One. The king issued a call to repentance and faithfulness; a call to be reconciled to God that wrath might be turned away. Hezekiah didn't express concern about Assyria or empty treasuries. Instead he cried out against sin, *"Because of our fathers' sin God's wrath came upon them; because we have walked in their ways—God's wrath is upon us"* (2 Chron. 29:8-9). Hezekiah recognized that though they had received a spoiled inheritance, it was their responsibility to return to God. His words cut to the root of the problem.

Perhaps you have received a spoiled inheritance. Maybe the struggles of life seem too great to conquer and you feel surrounded by unbeatable enemies. Maybe you are ready to quit in hopelessness at the condition of things in the Lord's House, but if you want to be obedient and escape the impending destruction, you must refuse to let circumstances determine your future. You must decide to turn back to God and encourage others to do the same.

Hezekiah **gathered** the priests and the Levites (Component #8) into the square on the east of the Temple. These men had been neglectful of their responsibilities in God's House, yet they also had sworn to love and serve the Lord. By definition, revival starts with believers. Hezekiah's call was sounded in the House of the Lord to the servants of the Lord who had become lukewarm and complacent. His cry was clear, *"Don't be negligent now, for the Lord has chosen you to stand before Him"* (2 Chron. 29:11). Hezekiah's message to the priests and Levites was that God had not chosen them to remain trapped under the generational curse of their fathers' behavior and beliefs, but to set a standard of holiness for a new generation.

The message to us is the same: Don't be negligent now. To be negligent means to be derelict, lax, remiss, slack, and careless. Do not be negligent—not now, because the pathetic powerlessness of defiled religion leads only to death and captivity. Like those in that court so long ago, the Lord has chosen us to stand before Him, be His ministers, and burn incense before Him (see 2 Chron. 29:11).

Some of the priests and Levites responded to Hezekiah's call—15, to be exact. Not exactly a tidal wave of revival, but it was a start. This small group began to exert an influence. They were able to involve other priests and Levites in the return to God (see 2 Chron. 29:12-15). The change in attitude and standards among the leadership of Judah had an effect. **High places were removed; sacred pillars and Asherah were broken down** (Component #15). In particular, it is recorded that Hezekiah broke in pieces Nehushtan, the bronze serpent that Moses had made (see 2 Kings 18:4). In the same way, a relatively small group of committed individuals with a good vision and strong leadership can begin a transformational return to God.

Hezekiah led the Levites in covenanting with the Lord (Component #9). It was a covenant of **consecration** (Component #13) (see 2 Chron. 29:10). Consecration means setting something aside, dedicating it to a specific use. Scripture gave directions for the initial consecration of priests. The process involved washing with water and anointing with blood and oil, but even after becoming a priest reconsecration was necessary at times. Moses warned, *"Let the priests who come near to the Lord consecrate themselves, or else the Lord will break out against them"* (Exod. 19:22). Our loving God is full of mercy, but because of His holiness we must be properly prepared to be in His presence.

Perhaps the clearest picture of consecration can be found in the teaching of the Nazirite vow in Numbers 6:1-21. The words *consecrate*, *dedicate*, *holy*, *separation*, and *separated* are used throughout this passage. The Nazirite vow was about radical commitment to God. The Nazirite vow could be life-long, as in the case of Samson, or it could be of shorter duration. It is also noteworthy that you didn't have to be a Levite, prophet, priest, or king to enter this time of intense relationship with God. You could be old or young, rich or poor, male or female. There were only three elements in the Nazirite vow:

- Abstinence from grapes and grape products, including wine and strong drink.

- No cutting of the hair.

- No touching of a dead person.

Each of these elements signifies spiritual commitment. Abstaining from grapes and alcohol illustrates finding our joy and intoxication in the Spirit of the Lord rather than earthly things. Letting the hair grow long represents surrender to the Lord, for the length and style of our hair often reflects our attitude, whether it be rebellious or submissive. In addition, in those days uncut hair was an obvious sign of a person under a vow to the Lord. Today, whether our hair is long or short, it should be clear that we are radically committed to the Lord. Touching a dead person was forbidden to Hebrews except in preparation of the body of a close relative for burial. Nazirites were not allowed even this. The prohibition about touching the dead was to prevent the spread of disease. In the same way, there are "dead" things that can defile us today when we "touch" them. Jesus taught us that the things that truly defile us are evil thoughts, murders, adulteries, fornications, thefts, false witness, and slanders, deeds of coveting and wickedness, as well as deceit, sensuality, envy, pride, and foolishness (see Matt. 15:19; Mark 7:22). We are to stay away from such things—no exceptions. Though some may proclaim freedom to "touch" these things, those committed to the Lord may not.

Consecration was not a one-time event. It was often repeated and deepened, as well as widened to include others in the revival accounts. We can learn more about consecration from observing other instances in Scripture when God's people took this important step:

- Joshua's command to Israel at the brink of crossing the Jordan River (see Josh. 3:5) shows that moving forward into what God has for us requires consecration.

- After Achan stole the items from Jericho, God spoke to Joshua again about consecration (see Josh. 7:13). When sin is in the camp, setting things right requires consecration.

- Samuel consecrated Jesse and his sons and invited them to the sacrifice (see 1 Sam. 16:5). When we desire that the Lord raise up leadership we must consecrate ourselves.

- David said to the Levites, *"Consecrate yourselves, both you and your relatives, that you may bring up the ark of the Lord God of Israel to the place that I have prepared for it"* (1 Chron. 15:12). When the presence of the Lord is needed, those who carry it must prepare by fresh consecration.

Hezekiah also commanded the priests and Levites to consecrate the House of the Lord. "Carry the uncleanness out from the holy place." In other words, let the House of the Lord be given back to Him and His service. In times of apostasy, the Temple became a repository for all sorts of things that shouldn't have been there. For example, in Nehemiah's time things belonging to Tobiah, one of Nehemiah's chief enemies, were moved into the Temple (see Neh. 13:4-5). God's things were moved out and Tobiah's belongings were put in their place. This illustrates that things that do not belong in church like gossip, backbiting, bitterness, and selfishness have taken the place of love, joy, praise, and power. Let's get rid of Tobiah's stuff! Let the habitation that God is building for Himself be undefiled! Like the task of the priests and Levites in Hezekiah's day, cleansing God's temple today is a challenge. Someone has said revival is like remodeling your house. It takes longer than you think; costs more than you planned, and makes a bigger mess than you thought it would.

The priests and Levites followed Hezekiah's godly leadership and **demonstrated obedience to human authority** (Component #5). It took eight days to consecrate themselves and another eight days to consecrate the House of the Lord. At the end of that time, they reported to the king that the whole house had been thoroughly cleansed (see 1 Chron. 29:17-19). The cleansing was done according to the commandment of the king **by the words of the Lord** (Component #3); that is to say they followed the directions in God's Word under Hezekiah's instruction (see 2 Chron. 30:12). In the same way, we must let Jesus, our King, guide us in the application of God's Word. He knows how the House of the Lord should be cleansed.

Hezekiah then assembled the princes of the city; it was a **gathering of a wider array of leaders** (Component #18). This expansion of the leadership group gave Hezekiah a chance to impart the vision of consecration to more people. They responded positively—going up to the House of the Lord and publicly confessed and **repented of sin** (Component #12). They further made things right with God by **sacrificing** (Component #10) sin and burnt offerings (see 1 Chron. 29:21-24).

The sacrifices were accompanied by **praise and worship** (Component #6). Hezekiah stationed the Levites in the House of the Lord with many instruments. When the burnt offering began, the song to the Lord also began and the whole assembly worshiped (see 2 Chron. 29:25). The singers sang, and the musicians played until the burnt offering was finished. The sacrifice consisted of seven each of bulls, lambs, and rams; it would have taken considerable time. Such was the attitude toward worship that at the completion of the offerings all who were present bowed down and worshiped. The king and the officials actually *ordered* the Levites to sing additional songs of David and Asaph to the Lord. They joyfully complied (see 2 Chron. 29:26-30). Then, to top it all off, additional sacrifices and offerings were made: 70 bulls, 100 rams, and 200 lambs. An additional 600 bulls and 3,000 sheep were set aside for the Lord. It was extravagant worship. The great influx of sacrifice overwhelmed the priests so that they were unable to skin all the burnt offerings; the Levites helped until more priests had consecrated themselves (see 2 Chron. 29:31-34).

Let us learn not to rush through our times of worship. Too many people see a worship service as the place where they had better find a good time or they won't return, and woe to the preacher who runs past the allotted number of minutes. The problem with this approach to worship is that the pursuit of happiness is the focus, when it should be the pursuit of holiness! These days, the concern seems to be what we get out of worship, instead of what God gets out of it. We want to be pleased, ourselves, more than we desire to please the Lord.

STAGE TWO REVIVAL (GOD RETURNS TO HIS PEOPLE)

Great joy (Result #3) arose. Hezekiah and all the people rejoiced over what God had prepared for the people, *"because the thing came about suddenly"* (2 Chron. 29:34). This sudden change in attitude and orientation is stunning. It seems to be a hallmark of true revival. Hezekiah and the people of Judah wanted others to experience the joy they had found so they invited all Israel to the **Passover celebration** (Result #10). They sent a proclamation throughout the land which read:

> O sons of Israel return to the Lord God of Abraham, Isaac and
> Israel, that He may return to those of you who escaped and are
> left from the hand of the kings of Assyria. Do not be like your
> fathers and your brothers, who were unfaithful to the Lord God
> of their fathers, so that He made them a horror, as you see. Do
> not stiffen your neck like your fathers, but yield to the Lord and
> enter His sanctuary which He has consecrated forever, and serve
> the Lord your God that His burning anger may turn away from
> you. For if you return to the Lord, your brothers and your sons

*will find compassion before those who led them captive and will return to this land. For the Lord your **God is gracious and compassionate, and will not turn His face away from you if you return to Him*** (2 Chronicles 30:1-9).

The message was strong but filled with grace and faith.

Some mocked the couriers and did not come to Jerusalem (see 2 Chron. 30:11). Opposition in the form of scorn and rejection of the consecration message is often the initial result when revival occurs.

Not all mocked however; **many did come to worship** (Result #4). Men of Asher, Manasseh, and Zebulun humbled themselves and came to Jerusalem (see 2 Chron. 30:11). God gave them one heart to obey their leaders according to the word of the Lord (see 2 Chron. 30:11). Where there is true revival, this supernatural sense of unity and a desire to obey can be found.

God poured out an amazing level of grace (Result #1). The newcomers had not purified themselves in preparation for the Passover, yet mercy was extended, and they ate. Hezekiah prayed for them saying:

"May the good Lord pardon everyone who prepares his heart to seek God, the Lord God of his fathers, though not according to the purification rules of the sanctuary." So the Lord heard Heze-kiah...and healed the people (2 Chronicles 30:18-20).

The influx of people required openness on the part of all. Acceptance and grace were extended to all who came; the newcomers were received with humility. The Lord's desire for the spirit of the law rather than the letter of the law was confirmed by an outpouring of healing.

A desire for holiness continued to grow in Judah. Remaining **idols were destroyed** (Result #12). The people cast them into the brook Kidron. In addition, more leaders consecrated themselves as they saw what God was doing. They were ashamed of themselves for holding back, so they, too, gave themselves to God (see 2 Chron. 30:14-17). The whole assembly decided to celebrate the feast another seven days (see 2 Chron. 30:22-23). A total of 2,000 bulls and 17,000 sheep were **sacrificed** (Result #7) and **great joy** (Result #3) filled Jerusalem. Nothing like this had happened in Jerusalem since the days of Solomon (see 2 Chron. 30:24-26).

The ministry of prayer and blessing was apparently more effective than usual. Scripture comments that the Levitical priests *"arose and blessed the people; and their voice was heard and their prayer came to His holy dwelling place, to heaven"* (see 2 Chron. 30:27). This is reminiscent of the Lord's promise in Numbers 6:22-27:

> *Speak to Aaron and to his sons, saying, "Thus you shall bless the sons of Israel. You shall say to them: the Lord bless you, and keep you; the Lord make His face shine on you, and be gracious to you; the Lord lift up His countenance on you, And give you peace." So they shall invoke My name on the sons of Israel,* ***and I then will bless them.***

The desire for holiness continued to spread. People went out from Jerusalem and broke down more idolatrous pillars. Asherim, high places and altars throughout all Judah and Benjamin, as well as in Ephraim and Manasseh, were destroyed (see 2 Chron. 31:1). This wonderful wave action of cleansing and consecration is an effect of true revival.

Worship (Result #2) was reestablished in the Temple and **ministry was set in order** (Result #6). *"Hezekiah appointed divisions of the priests and the Levites...for burnt offerings and for peace offerings, to minister and to give thanks and to praise in the gates of the camp of the Lord"* (2 Chron. 31:2-3). In revival, wise leadership will bring order to people willing to serve, making ministry effective.

Tithing (Result #8) was reinstituted (see 2 Chron. 31:3-4). As soon as the command to tithe was given, the sons of Israel began to bring in the tithe. Items were consecrated to the Lord and placed in heaps. It was a process that took four months. So abundant was the giving that when Hezekiah saw the piles, he questioned the priests and the Levites about it. Azariah, the chief priest of the house of Zadok, said to him, *"Since the contributions began to be brought into the house of the Lord, we have had enough to eat with plenty left over, for the Lord has blessed His people, and this great quantity is left over"* (2 Chron. 31:5-10). Giving to the Lord was so great that oversight of this area had to be expanded. Room was prepared for the offerings and authority delegated to individuals to care for the abundance (see 2 Chron. 31:11-21).

There was another miraculous intervention (Result #1). Sennacherib, king of Assyria, invaded the land and besieged some of Judah's cities (see 2 Chron. 32:1). God allowed the attack but He did not allow the enemy to triumph. Instead, it is Sennacherib's defeat that is recorded with the catastrophic and unexplained loss of 185,000 soldiers in one night (see 2 Kings 18-20; Isa. 36).

REVIVAL THEME

This revival turned on Hezekiah's challenge to the priests and Levites to, "Consecrate yourselves, now!" His words must have reverberated in their souls. He called them back to their destiny. So must there be a call to the Church, today's priests and Levites. We need to again be challenged to truly give ourselves to the Lord.

ENDNOTE

1. A narrative based on First Chronicles 29 and Second Kings 18:4.

Points to Ponder

1. Judah was struggling with the spiritual, financial, and political consequences of turning from the Lord. What does this say to us about our present-day national situation?

2. Hezekiah's father left him this spoiled inheritance. Nevertheless, Hezekiah became a strong godly leader and led Judah back to God in a great revival. What qualities in strong godly leaders do you most admire?

3. Hezekiah told the priests and Levites, "Don't be negligent now, for the Lord has chosen you to stand before Him, to minister to Him, and to be His ministers and burn incense." How does this urgent command relate to Christians today?

4. Hezekiah's revival was among the most powerful of all the Old Testament awakenings. In your view, what were the key factors that led to this wonderful time of refreshing?

Chapter 10

THE JOSIAH REVIVAL
TRUTH REDISCOVERED

THE BOOK[1]

A passion for the Lord was burning in Josiah, the king of Judah. Though he was still a young man, he was determined to revitalize worship of the Lord in the nation. It disturbed him greatly that the stately Temple constructed in Solomon's time had been neglected in recent generations. That awesome edifice, now more than 250 years old, desperately needed structural repairs. Josiah summoned Shaphan, his chief of staff, and commanded, "See to it that the best of materials are used.... It's not right that the Lord's house should languish uncared for. I will not have it so!"

Josiah had earlier reproved the people for no longer bringing their tithes and offerings. They had responded with an outpouring of provision. The time had come to correct the problems at the grand old building. Armed with the king's command and a fortified treasury, Shaphan diligently began to carry out the king's orders. Under Shaphan's direction and the supervision of the high priest Hilkiah, stone was quarried to rebuild some of the old walls and timber was procured from Lebanon to make new beams. Thus, repairs to the magnificent structure began.

Shaphan was inspecting the progress one day when Hilkiah pulled him aside. With great excitement the high priest told him, "I have just found the Book of the Law! It was hidden in the wall!" Shaphan was stunned, speechless. The recent kings of Judah had been Baal worshipers and among the most wicked of all Judah's monarchs. They had even attempted to destroy all copies of the Word of the Lord. Some unknown faithful priest must have hidden the precious manuscripts behind a masonry wall to preserve them from destruction.

Hilkiah took Josiah's chief of staff by the arm and led him into a storeroom outside of which the priest had posted two Levites as guards. There, a table was set against a wall that had some stones removed from it; and on the table lay a set of ancient scrolls. Shaphan slowly took in the sight along with a deep breath. He approached the table with reverence. His hands trembled as he gently touched the beautifully lettered manuscripts. Realizing the old parchments were more valuable than he could even imagine, he bowed, and whispered softly in prayer, "Lord God, how good You are."

Shaphan and Hilkiah were tempted to examine the scrolls but quickly agreed that they should take the precious writings to the king immediately. They carefully packed the treasures into a soft cloth bag that Shaphan scooped into his arms. As they hurried to the palace Hilkiah said, "*I'll* tell the king what I found." Shaphan nodded in agreement.

Shaphan could hardly wait to see the king's face when the high priest told him the good news. Shaphan had grown up with Josiah. They shared a deep friendship and he, too, loved the God of Israel. Shaphan marveled as he hurried along, "These words were written at the command of the Lord! No one has read them for generations!" The king's official and the high priest hurriedly climbed the steps to the palace and strode down the hall to the paneled room where kings of Judah held court.

Josiah lounged on the elaborate throne eating dates from a bowl at his side. The two men approached and waited for the king to acknowledge them, which Josiah did with a cordial nod and a question, "When will the renovations be complete?" Shaphan reported with a grin, "The workmen are making good progress, O king." Hilkiah quickly nodded, "We expect the repairs will be completed within 30 days." Josiah accepted the report and said, "Schedule a celebration for the following month." The two men readily agreed. The king dismissed them with a wave of his hand and turned his attention back to the food before him. But Shaphan and Hilkiah remained standing in front of the throne, not backing away as was customary. Josiah stared at his trusted advisor and the high priest and arched a puzzled eyebrow at the excited smiles on their faces. Hilkiah cleared his throat and began grandly, "We brought something to show you that I found…", but the excitement was too much for Shaphan. "Hilkiah found the Book of the Law!" he blurted, unable to contain the news any longer. He raised the cloth bag in both hands and literally jumped slightly as he repeated, "He *found* the Book of the Law!" Hilkiah frowned at Shaphan, momentarily irritated by the interruption. But joy overwhelmed all irritation, and he added with a wide smile, "It was hidden in the wall of the Temple!"

Stunned silence filled the large room. Sixty years had passed since the God-breathed record was last seen, let alone read, by anyone. Hopes that a copy of the ancient Scriptures still survived had long ago faded. The king abandoned his dates, straightened on his throne, and simply commanded, "Read!" With a sudden scurry, attendants brought a table on which to place the contents of the bag, and a chair. News of the discovery spread quickly in the palace, and officials and courtiers gathered in growing numbers. They stood or sat on the marble floor as Shaphan and Hilkiah took turns reading from the old scrolls for the next few hours. Everyone listened, enthralled by the account of creation, the history of God's faithfulness to the early fathers, Israel's slavery and mighty deliverance from Egypt. As the men read the laws and instructions from the Lord himself, no one spoke or moved. When evening fell and daylight faded, lamps were lit so they could continue.

Finally, they finished. All eyes turned to the king. Josiah, staggered at the righteous requirements of the Law, rose from where he had slumped on the throne. He walked to his friend and chief of staff, who stood as the king approached. Josiah grasped Shaphan's shoulders and said with intensity, "We are far from the Lord." Josiah groaned, "There is so much we have done wrong." Staring at Hilkiah, King Josiah said, "We have neglected the Lord and His House. We have worshiped other gods. We have not taught our children to honor and fear the Lord." Tears ran down his face. He ripped the fine silk shirt he wore and fell to his knees on the marble floor. The presence of the Lord was almost tangible; everyone in the hall followed the young king's example. This time of spontaneous repentance lasted well into the night.

Though it was late when he rose from the floor, Josiah immediately appointed a delegation to go to the house of Huldah the prophetess. Through this delegation, Josiah pleaded with Huldah:

Inquire of the Lord for us. Great is the wrath of the Lord which is poured out on us because our fathers have not observed the word of the Lord, to do according to all that is written in this book (2 Chronicles 34:21).

Carrying torches through the dark streets of Jerusalem, the small group sought out the house of the godly old woman. After listening to them, she gave them this message for the king:

Thus says the Lord, the God of Israel, "Behold, I am bringing evil on this place and on its inhabitants. Because they have forsaken Me and have burned incense to other gods; therefore My wrath will be poured out on this place and it shall not be quenched." But also say to him, Thus says the Lord God of Israel, "because your heart was tender and you humbled yourself before God when you heard His words, and wept before Me, I truly have heard you," declares the Lord (2 Chronicles 34:24-27).

The next day King Josiah gathered the people of Jerusalem, from the greatest to the least, in the court of the Temple. He read in their hearing all the words of the book that was found in the House of the Lord and led the great throng in making a covenant with the Lord to walk after Him and keep His commandments with all their heart and soul.

THE SETTING FOR REVIVAL

Like Joash, the boy-king of an earlier generation, Josiah came to the throne at a very early age. He had all he needed in the natural. But his childhood was filled with turmoil. Josiah's father, Amon, had been a complete failure as a monarch. He was a Baal worshiper and only reigned two years. Amon was so wicked his servants conspired against him and put him to death. The people of Judah then executed all the conspirators, and then crowned eight-year-old Josiah king of Judah. A measure of strife and division undoubtedly remained in the kingdom—not a stable situation for a child to take the helm of a nation. For many reasons, Josiah could have had spiritual and emotional problems in his life. Yet, he did not allow negative things in his background to keep him from serving the Lord wholeheartedly.

STAGE ONE REVIVAL (GOD'S PEOPLE RETURN TO HIM)

Despite the bad example of his father, Josiah became **a strong godly leader** (Component #1) and one of the best kings of Judah. We don't know much about his early years, but at the age of 16 we do know that he began to seek the Lord. At 20, he launched a war on idols (2 Chron. 33:21-25). After two generations of Baal worshipers, Judah had a king who loved the Lord. Josiah could have continued down the path of destruction set by his father; instead, he chose to follow the Lord (2 Chron. 34:2-3). Unlike Joash, Josiah did not have a godly mentor to guide him. Apparently he initiated this personal and national revival on his own.

Many people have had parents who were poor role models, but having bad examples doesn't dictate our choices. Maybe your family has not had born-again Christians in it, and you're going to have to break new ground with the Lord. The lesson of Josiah is that spiritual heritage doesn't determine our spiritual destiny in God. One generation can make a difference!

Josiah led the people in zealously **cleansing Judah and Jerusalem of idols** (Component #15). He removed the high places of Baal worship, the evil Asherim, and the other carved images. Under his direction, the people of Judah burned the bones of the Canaanite priests on their own altars, then tore down those altars, ground them to powder, and scattered the remains on the graves of those who had sacrificed to the Baals (see 2 Chron. 34:3-7). Topheth (maybe the worst idol of all)—where children were sacrificed to the god Molech—was also destroyed (see 2 Kings 23:4-10).

Josiah then decided to repair the Temple and restore it to the service of the Lord (see 2 Chron. 34:8). This was a fateful decision that would bring great change, for the Temple held a hidden treasure. The king commanded that all the vessels made for Baal, Asherah, and other Canaanite idols be brought out of the Lord's House and burned. He also removed the houses of the male cult prostitutes that were in the Temple. Josiah also **reinstituted tithing** (Component #8), ensuring that Hilkiah the high priest had the funds he needed to renovate the Temple (see 2 Chron. 34:9-13).

Josiah's story illustrates that when you start seeking the Lord, eventually you will develop a passionate **concern for the House of God** (Component #11). Some say they love the Lord but have been hurt within the Church; thereafter, they want nothing to do with organized religion. How can this be, given that Jesus loves His Bride and never gives up on her?

We should never underestimate the blessings associated with giving to the Lord and His House. As God's people gave, the construction and repair process moved forward, eventually leading to the discovery of "the Book" (see 2 Chron. 34:14-18). Giving to the Lord in the context of the local church is one of the disciplines God will use to guide us to truth. Josiah provides a wise example in his love for the Lord and His House.

We must give Josiah a great deal of credit. He came to power in a difficult time in Judah's history. He was part of a dysfunctional family and, at the time he began instituting reforms, he didn't have the Bible for a guide. In spite of these handicaps, Josiah destroyed many idols and started a building program to renovate the House of the Lord.

When the Book of the Law was found, **the entire nation returned to God's Word** as the rule for faith and practice (Component #3). Interestingly, the Book of the Law was lost in the House of God. It had been hidden and covered up. Some churches today have a similar problem. If you visit a church and you don't "find the Book," you are clearly in the wrong church. When the Book was found, Josiah and all Judah accepted its authoritative voice. This recognition of the God-breathed message as divine communication can be seen in every generation when people return to the Lord. Paul said to the Thessalonians:

[We] *constantly thank God that when you received the word of God which you heard from us, you accepted it not as the word of men, but for what it really is, the word of God, which also performs its work in you who believe* (1 Thessalonians 2:12).

The Bible is not a book of magic, philosophy, psychology, or social science. It is a record of God's interaction with man through the ages and those interactions reveal His person, plan, and purpose. We do a great disservice to ourselves by neglecting this magnificent document! We need to "find the Book" that is unique in its teachings, fulfilled prophecy, accuracy, and power. We need to find the Book!

Finding the Bible is a watershed experience in people's lives. The phrase "finding the Bible" implies the recognition that it is a revelation of truth from God, and the corresponding acceptance of the Bible's content as authoritative. Whenever this happens, God's Word rocks the foundations of our lives. This is true even for those who have striven to live a good life and to do righteous works. "Finding the Book" means that whatever we previously considered to be truth is now subject to review and change. What we considered to be correct and incorrect now becomes subject to the standard of a loving but holy God expressed through His written Word. We may find ourselves emotionally and spiritually undone in this process, as did King Josiah. Certainly, the orientation of our lives will shift dramatically because this recognition of the authority of God's Word demolishes religious strongholds and rewrites our standards.

I have witnessed that those who "find the Book" continue on with the Lord. Those who don't, slip away, even though they may have had a powerful experience with God. Without the sure guide of Heaven's handbook, believers are vulnerable to the unceasing attacks of the world and the kingdom of darkness.

When the king heard the words of the Law, he tore his clothes. Hearing the Word of God led to **repentance** (Component #13). As he heard

Shaphan and Hilkiah read, Josiah must have been thinking: "If this is true, we are in serious trouble." Josiah also realized the people of Judah would need help in understanding the importance of what he had been hearing. So the king commanded Hilkiah, Ahikam the son of Shaphan, Abdon the son of Micah, Shaphan the scribe, and Asaiah the king's servant, to inquire of the Lord at the house of Huldah the prophetess. The news from Huldah was mixed. She said, "Judgment is coming because of all the evil in the land." However, there was good news also. The woman of God sent this message back to the young king:

> *"Because your heart was tender and you humbled yourself before God when you heard His words against this place and against its inhabitants, and because you humbled yourself before Me, tore your clothes and wept before Me, I truly have heard you," declares the Lord* (2 Chronicles 34:27).

Josiah then **gathered the elders** (Component #18) of Judah. The entire nation **assembled in unity** (Component #4) as well, and went up to the House of the Lord to hear the Word of God read aloud (see 2 Chron. 34:29-30). Afterward, everyone joined the king in **making a covenant** with the Lord (Component #9) to keep His commandments (see 2 Chron. 34:31). As Judah began to obey the God of their fathers, societal transformation occurred: Standards of conduct changed, wickedness was removed, and righteousness was built up. Josiah removed *"the abominations from all the lands belonging to the sons of Israel."* Throughout Josiah's lifetime, the kingdom of Judah did not turn from following the Lord (see 2 Chron. 34:32-33).

Like Judah, America has removed the Bible from public discourse. Many of our leaders and officials do not know its tenets. If they do hear or read portions of Scripture, few seek out anyone who can help them understand the import. The grievous and tragic results of hiding "the Book" in the House of the Lord, and the ignorance of God's ways that ensues, were fully apparent to Josiah and those he ruled. Banishing God and His truth from government and marketplace is folly. Judah had fallen from power and prosperity and was in dire danger. Though God's judgment was still coming, Josiah led his people back to God for a time. Today we face turmoil and uncertainty. May we also rediscover "the Book" as a nation and not be ashamed to read it publicly and privately for wisdom and direction.

Josiah organized and encouraged the priests to serve the Lord and the people (see 2 Chron. 35:2-5). *The priests were consecrated and sacrifices were made* (Components #13 and #10). A part of this consecration process was the observation of **Passover** (Result #10). Josiah donated lambs and young goats numbering 30,000, plus 3,000 bulls. The freewill offerings totaled another 7,600 from the flocks and 800 bulls. All the priests and Levites helped in the observance and everyone received ministry (see 2 Chron. 35:6-9).

Praise and worship (Component #6) were lifted to the Lord in the Temple again. The singers, the sons of Asaph, were stationed according to the commands of David, Asaph, Heman, and Jeduthun the king's seer. Nothing like it had been seen since the days of Samuel (see 2 Chron. 35:15). A massive spiritual revolution was proceeding in an amazing fashion as true revival burst forth in the kingdom.

Tragically, the awakening ended prematurely without a full-blown stage two revival when the people of Judah lost their godly leader. Josiah entered a battle he was not supposed to be in. Neco, Egypt's pharaoh, marched north through the land. His goal was to make war on the Babylonians, but Josiah went out to engage him. Neco sent messengers to him, saying:

> *What have we to do with each other, O King of Judah? I am not*
> *coming against you today but against the house with which I am*
> *at war, and God has ordered me to hurry. Stop for your own sake*

from interfering with God who is with me, so that He will not
destroy you (2 Chronicles 35:20-27).

Despite this warning and plea, Josiah would not turn away. He died in
the battle and was buried with honors in Jerusalem. Without his dynamic
leadership, the nation soon faltered in their pursuit of God. Judah fell back
into a spiritual darkness from which they would not recover for another
century.

REVIVAL THEME

The great truth of discovery, or rediscovery, of the treasure that is the
written Word of almighty God is the theme of the Josiah revival. The fact
that in Josiah's time "the Book" lay hidden in God's House warns us to
take care that the Bible is not only *in* the Church but that its transforming
truths are revealed to people. If the Bible is merely present—not read,
understood, and applied—it might as well be hidden in the wall; its power
is concealed and its authority is muted.

ENDNOTE

1.   A narrative based on Second Chronicles 34 and 35.

POINTS TO PONDER

1. The "Book" had been hidden in the House of the Lord. How did this happen in Josiah's time? How does it happen now?

2. Josiah decided to renovate the House of the Lord. Isn't it interesting that when we realize that God's House is in disrepair and begin a renovation, this renovation will lead us to "find the Book?" When we find the Book, we will be able to restore the true House of the Lord.

3. Finding the Book rocked Josiah's world. Has the Book rocked your world? In what ways?

4. Where and when did you find the Book?

Chapter 11

THE ZERUBBABEL REVIVAL
REBUILDING THE TEMPLE

SHOUTS OF GRACE[1]

With the help of stone masons using levers, Zerubbabel and Jeshua pushed hard…and the large limestone block ground the last handbreadth into place, matching beautifully with the stones on either side. The massive block was the capstone of the Temple. Zerubbabel, Jerusalem's governor, gave it a loving pat, a long look, and then stepped up onto the stone. Jeshua, the high priest, joined him. It was a breathtaking 20-cubit drop to the pavement below. From their vantage point, these two leaders of Jerusalem could see the throng below and the flames burning in the altar ready for the sacrifices that would be offered this day. Zerubbabel lifted his hands to the heavens and the crowd in the court cheered, "Grace! Grace!" The shouts made him smile. He turned and looked down at Zechariah and Haggai, the prophets, who stood on the roof nearby, and spoke loudly to Zechariah, "It is as you prophesied. They are shouting, 'Grace!'" The prophet grinned widely and lifted his reply over the jubilant sounds of worship, "The Lord brings His Word to pass!"

Zerubbabel looked to the east over the Kidron valley. The Mount of Olives was lush with groves of olive trees. To the south, a thin plume of dusky smoke rose into the clear sky from the garbage dump in the valley of Hinnom. Looking to the west and north, he could see the city of Jerusalem, still recovering from being leveled 90 years earlier by the Babylonians. There were still no city walls, and she was undoubtedly a pale shadow of what she had been in the days of the kings.

The Temple on which he stood was not as large or ornate as Solomon's had been, but it stood strong. Zerubbabel put his hand on Jeshua's shoulder. The two men were like brothers. This day was a day they had planned and labored for most of their adult lives. Memories flooded both men as they savored the moment. Twenty years earlier they had led almost 50,000 people several hundred miles westward from Persia to the City of David. The altar in the court below was the first thing they rebuilt. Its completion and use had galvanized everyone to begin rebuilding the Temple. They had been able to lay the foundation of the Temple before opposition from the surrounding peoples stalled construction for more than 15 years. But now, finally, the Lord's House was finished and a great victory realized.

Zerubbabel asked his friend, "Do you remember when we laid the foundation?" Jeshua nodded, "The trumpets and cymbals…the worship was tremendous!" Zerubbabel added, "We sang, 'He is good, for His lovingkindness is upon Israel forever,' again and again." "And then we all shouted with a great shout!" responded the priest, "We were so excited!" He paused and then continued, "But the older men wept, thinking of Solomon's Temple." "Yes," said the Governor thoughtfully, "but the old Temple was gone. We had to move on!" The two men stepped off the capstone back onto the roof. There they embraced Haggai and Zechariah, who had encouraged them so much over the years of rebuilding effort.

Later, after the ceremony of dedication in the courtyard, the four reclined at the evening meal in Zerubbabel's house. The governor reminisced, "It was so discouraging when the soldiers came in and stopped the work by force. That was the low point. I needed that encouragement you gave me, Zechariah!" The prophet nodded, "The word about you laying the foundation *and* the capstone amid shouts of grace was as clear as any I've ever received from the Lord."

Zerubbabel's eyes filled with tears as he thought of how the Lord had brought them through so much difficulty to a great achievement. He turned to Haggai and asked something he had often thought about, "What did the Lord mean, 'The latter glory of this house will be greater than the former, and in this place I will give peace?'" Haggai didn't reply immediately. He was old enough to remember the magnificence of Solomon's Temple and had often pondered the very prophecy to which Zerubbabel referred. He stroked his beard and said in measured tones, "I believe it has to do with Messiah!" Their conversation ceased for several minutes as they pondered this thought. Zerubbabel then asked with intensity, "He will come to our Temple?" The other men nodded almost in unison, "He must come," Jeshua whispered.

A little more than 500 years later an old man was walking in the colonnade of the Temple. Although it was called "Herod's temple," (because he had refurbished and expanded it) at its heart, the Temple was the structure Zerubbabel had built. The old man with the kindly face and snowy hair saw a young couple coming toward him. The mother carried a newborn. The little family was not an unusual sight in the House of the Lord. All first-born males had to be presented at the Temple; but for some reason the old man stopped and stared at them. He broke off his prayer and made his way over as the little family waited for a priest. Drawing near, excitement bubbled in his heart. It only took one look at the face of the infant boy lying in His mother's arms and Simeon gasped. With trembling hands, Simeon took the baby in his arms and praised God, saying:

Now Lord, You are releasing Your bond-servant to depart in peace, according to Your word; for my eyes have seen Your salvation, which You have prepared in the presence of all peoples, a light of revelation to the gentiles and the glory of Your people Israel (Luke 2:29-32).

THE SETTING FOR REVIVAL

The theme for this revival is Israel's return from captivity to rebuild the Temple. It illustrates the restoration of liberated worship in the Church. Most of the nation of Israel had been taken captive to Babylon. The scene for the homecoming to Jerusalem was set with the accession of Cyrus to the throne of Persia. Two hundred years earlier, Isaiah had prophetically called the Persian king by name, stating that under him the Jews would return and rebuild Jerusalem (see Isa. 44:26-28,45:1,13). The time arrived and the Lord raised Cyrus up and stirred him to send a proclamation throughout his kingdom, saying: "Whoever there is among you of the Lord's people, may his God be with him! Let him go up to Jerusalem which is in Judah and rebuild the house of the Lord, the God of Israel" (Ezra 1:3). Israel's return to Jerusalem in 536 B.C. also fulfilled the prophecy given by Jeremiah concerning seventy years of captivity (see Jer. 1:1-3; 25:11-12; 29:10). At the time, Daniel was still a force in Cyrus's court and may have shown him these prophecies. If so, it is not surprising that the Persian king had a high level of respect for the God of the Hebrews.

The Israelites were offered the opportunity to return to God's place and God's plan. We, too, are offered that same opportunity on a spiritual plane. We have the task of leading God's people back to Him and building up worship.

STAGE ONE REVIVAL (GOD'S PEOPLE RETURN TO HIM)

There were two men who rose to the challenge posed by Cyrus's offer. Their names were Zerubbabel and Jeshua. They were key **strong and godly leaders** in this revival (Component #1). It is notable that this revival was led by two men in a strong partnership. As such, it is an exception to the rule of one strong godly leader. Zerubbabel was the grandson of Jehoiachin—the last king of Judah. Jeshua was the great-grandson of

Hilkiah, the high priest who helped King Josiah lead Judah into revival. Jeshua now held the office of high priest. Together, Zerubbabel and Jeshua would rebuild the Temple destroyed by Nebuchadnezzar. It would take 20 years and much heartache and labor amid great opposition. We don't hear much about Zerubbabel and Jeshua, but they were champions for God.

God's people had **a shared vision** (Component #2). Many of them had been longing to return to Jerusalem for generations (Ezra 1:5). By coming under Zerubbabel and Jeshua's leadership, **they demonstrated obedience to authority** (Component #3), for the Jews faced a choice in regard to going back to Israel. Some of the people couldn't wait to return—primarily, those from the tribes of Judah and Benjamin. Along with the priests and Levites, they heard the call and responded. A much smaller number from the remnants of the northern tribes joined in. When the word of revival begins to spread, usually those who have been living closest to the Lord are first to respond. Even so, the whole company returning to Jerusalem numbered barely 50,000. Many more of God's people chose to remain in Babylon, which seems strange given the great opportunity and privilege facing them. The offer was extended to every Israelite and King Cyrus supplied provisions for all. An offering for the building project was also given, and maybe most important of all, Cyrus returned to them the articles from Solomon's Temple that Nebuchadnezzar had carried away (see Ezra 2:4-7). Except when Israel was released from Egypt, we don't know of any other captive people who were blessed with such an opportunity. It could only have been a move of God.

Those who chose to remain in Babylon had their reasons. Some, undoubtedly, were comfortable in Persia. It was the superpower of the day and life would have been affluent and easy. Many were deeply involved with the social, political, or business life of Babylon. Leaving positions of power and prestige after 70 years would have been difficult. Not all their friends and family would have been willing to go. Some may have thought the venture was too dangerous or were afraid of failure. Interestingly, those who stayed behind did fail. They failed to see the enormity of the opportunity they had been given. They failed to enter into the destiny God had for them.

These reasons correlate to why many "Christians" do not choose to return to the Lord with a whole heart. Those who remained in Persia thought it would cost them too much to leave, in one way or another. It is true that there is a cost in returning to the Lord.

When we are in spiritual captivity, we can begin to believe that life as we know it is normative for Christians. But God has invited us to return to Him and live a different life. Lot is an example of those who become corrupt because they stay where they shouldn't have been. "While he *lingered*, the men (angels) took hold of his hand...and...brought him out and set him outside the city" (see Gen. 19:16). Lot was so comfortable in Sodom, he did not want to leave. The angels basically had to drag him out of town. His wife loved Sodom so much, she couldn't resist looking back. As a result, she was turned into a pillar of salt. Later, from an incestuous relationship with his daughters, Lot produced two ungodly lines called the Moabites and Ammonites (see Gen. 19:36-38). These people often attacked the Israelites. The lesson is simple: Christians must separate themselves from the world. If we do not, we will eventually become like the world and create problems for ourselves.

When those who did return to Jerusalem arrived, they **willingly offered** their substance to restore the House of God (Component #8). In all, they gave to the treasury 61,000 gold drachmas, 5,000 silver minas, and 100 priestly garments (see Ezra. 2:68-69). Those who truly love God love His House and His spiritual leaders, and freely give to maintain both.

The day came when the people **gathered together** "as one man" (Component #4) in Jerusalem (see Ezra 3:1). They came together for a common purpose—to do the work of rebuilding the Temple. After two years of preparation, they began work on the Temple by laying its foundation.

This wasn't the time for individualism; rather, this was an important time to be involved in the corporate life of faith. I can't tell you how often I've heard people say, "I don't have to attend church to be a Christian. I can worship God in my heart." This statement is true...to a point: nothing you can do, nothing you can join, can make you right with God. The Bible makes it abundantly clear that Jesus is the only way; no one comes to the Father except through Him. But the Bible also places immense value on the Church gathering together to work and worship. Let me refer you to the Book of Hebrews.

> Let us hold fast the confession of our hope without wavering, for He who promised is faithful; and let us consider how to stimulate one another to love and good deeds, not forsaking our own assembling together, as is the habit of some, but encouraging one another; and all the more, as you see the day drawing near (Hebrews 10:23-25).

Those who truly hunger for revival will come together as one in loving unity.

There was **a return to the Word** (Component #3). Scripture says Jeshua, Zerubbabel, and their brothers arose and built the altar of God, "*as it is written in the Law of Moses, the man of God*" (Ezra 3:2). In other words, they built the altar according to the instructions in the Word. During all the years in Babylon, the people had no altar; thus, they had no clear access to God and no assurance of forgiveness. Their disobedience had taken the altar away and broken their fellowship with God.

Now **they offered sacrifices** (Component #10). Fear of the people of the lands drove them to offer burnt offerings on the altar to the Lord morning and evening (see Ezra 3:2-3). They sacrificed daily to the Lord because they were afraid of their enemies. But at least they did offer worship. They must not be despised because they sacrificed under political pressure. When opposition comes, we will either draw close to the Lord or be pushed away from Him. Sometimes fear of the enemy can be overwhelming. In those moments, we must do what the Jews did. We must rebuild the altar of sacrifice. We must return to the cross of Christ where His blood was shed for our sins. This is our only hope. Often, we wonder at such times if God will take us back and rise in our defense. He will, but we will never know until we take those steps.

They separated from the world (Component #11). They celebrated the Feast of Booths, which was a holiday commemorating Israel's deliverance from Egypt and their wilderness sojourn when they had no houses (see Ezra 4:4-7). Turning from the world brought a focus on the Temple.

Ministry was set in order and **work began on God's House** (Components #7 and #16). Jeshua, with his sons, brothers, and other priests, stood united with the sons of Judah and the Levites to oversee the workmen in the Temple of God (see Ezra. 4:9). Thus, the foundation of the Temple was laid.

God builds us up when we renew our commitment to the foundation of Christ, and Christ only, in our lives. There is only one foundation. *"No man can lay a foundation other than the one which is laid, which is Jesus Christ"* (1 Cor. 3:11). People who know how to build know that the foundation is the most important part of a building because the foundation determines its size, shape, and strength. If the foundation is laid correctly, then whatever is built on top of it, whether it's a single-story house or a skyscraper, will stand.

Praise and worship were lifted to the Lord (Component #6). When the builders laid the foundation stones, priests and Levites stood in holy apparel with trumpets and cymbals. They sang, praising and giving thanks to the Lord, saying, "He is good, for His lovingkindness is upon Israel forever." Many shouted aloud for joy at the occasion (see Ezra. 4:10). However, many of the old men who had seen the first Temple wept with a loud voice—so much so it was difficult to distinguish the sound of the shout of joy from the sound of the weeping (see Ezra. 3:11-13). The old people looked back and wept. The young people looked ahead and rejoiced.

Some of us have experienced great times with God in the past. Don't let those memories cause you to miss out on the excitement of what God is doing now. Our past is God's to deal with. Treasure the good things, let go of the bad, and go on with the Lord.

The first wave of **opposition** arose (Result #15) at this point. Word will spread quickly when you start to rebuild the House of the Lord. The enemies of Judah and Benjamin heard with dismay that the people of the exile were constructing a Temple to the Lord God of Israel. So they tried to derail the project in several ways:

- **Infiltration**: Like the Jebusites in Joshua's day, the enemies of the Lord's work used deceit. They approached Zerubbabel saying to him, *"Let us build with you, for we, like you, seek your God"* (Ezra. 4:1). They claimed to worship the same God, but there were fundamental differences. Zerubbabel was wise in his response. He refused their offer (see Ezra 4:2). If their plan was not outright sabotage, the result would still have been disastrous; true revival demands no admixture of the worship of other gods.

- **Intimidation**: The Canaanite inhabitants of the land discouraged and frightened the people of Judah in order to stop them from building (see Ezra 4:4).

- **Litigation**: They hired lawyers against them to frustrate their counsel in the courts of Cyrus and Darius, kings of Persia (see Ezra 4:5).

- **Accusation**: They said the Jews were rebellious lawbreakers and wouldn't pay their taxes. That kind of accusation will get the attention of any politician! Finally, Artaxerxes, the Persian king at the time, issued a decree to halt construction. The work on the Temple was stopped by force and remained stalled for some 15 years (see Ezra. 4:17-24).

Prophets exhorted Zerubbabel, Jeshua, and the people to resume work (Component #15). God took special note of Haggai and Zechariah's support of the leaders (see Ezra 5:2). The related passages in the Books of *Haggai and Zechariah should be required reading for those who consider themselves prophets.* Pastors and ministry leaders need the prophetic ministry, but so often it serves to tear down rather than encourage and strengthen leaders. Haggai and Zechariah got it right. Haggai's exhortations included reproof and encouragement:

1. *"This people says, 'The time has not come, even the time for the house of the Lord to be rebuilt.'"* They were saying that nothing could be done at the time. Through Haggai, the Lord begged to differ, *"Is it time for you yourselves to dwell in your paneled houses while this house lies desolate?"* (Hag. 1:2-4). We must pay attention to marriage, family, and business. But let's face it, the devil and life will make sure it is never a convenient time to rebuild the Lord's House.

2. The Lord exhorted them to reevaluate:

   Consider your ways! You have sown much, but harvest little; you eat, but there is not enough to be satisfied; you drink, but there is not enough to become drunk; you put on clothing, but no one is warm enough; and he who earns, earns wages to put into a purse with holes (Haggai 1:5-8).

Difficulties often come our way because of wrong priorities. God wanted them to get busy on building the Temple despite the difficulties they were experiencing. *"Go up to the mountains, bring wood and rebuild the temple that I may be pleased with it and be glorified"* (Hag. 1:8). The implication was that when we put God first, our needs will be met.

3. Work began again on God's House. Honoring God through obedience earned high praise from Haggai: *"Zerubbabel...and Jeshua...with all the remnant of the people, obeyed the voice of the Lord...and the people showed reverence for the Lord"* (Hag. 1:12).

4. God understands how difficult it can be to gather up strength in situations where the work of the Lord has stopped and discouragement reigns. He reassured the people of Judah of His presence: *"I am with you"* (Hag. 1:13).

5. He also warned them not to compare this time with the past. *"'Who is left among you who saw this temple in its former glory? And how do you see it now? Does it not seem to you like nothing in comparison?"* (Hag. 2:3) They needed to start afresh, regardless of what glory they had seen or from what height they had fallen.

6. God exhorted them to simply be brave and work: *"'Take courage, Zerubbabel,' declares the Lord, 'take courage also, Jeshua son of Jehozadak, the high priest, and all you people of the land take courage,' declares the Lord, 'and work'"* (Hag. 2:4). We wish that God would do it all for us and that there would be no need for us to courageously go forward when the odds are stacked against us. But this is not God's means of developing

His people. While the work on Calvary is finished, there is still labor in the Lord's kingdom to accomplish.

7. The Lord again reaffirmed He would not leave them in their hour of need and testing: *"As for the promise which I made you when you came out of Egypt, My Spirit is abiding in your midst; do not fear"* (Hag. 2:5).

8. He told them He was still in control of all things: *"Once more in a little while, I am going to shake the heavens and the earth, the sea also and the dry land"* (Hag. 2:6).

9. God then revealed a precious truth to these weary workers:

    "I will fill this house with glory. The latter glory of this house will be greater than the former..., and in this place I will give peace," declares the Lord of hosts (Haggai 2:7,9).

It was a prophetic statement concerning the Messiah coming to Zerubbabel's Temple not the more beautiful structure built by Solomon.

God also encouraged Zerubbabel and Jeshua through the ministry of Zechariah:

1. Zechariah related a vision he had seen of Jeshua:

    [God] *showed me Jeshua the high priest standing before the angel of the Lord, and Satan standing at his right hand to accuse him. The Lord said to Satan, "The Lord rebuke you, Satan! Indeed, the Lord who has chosen Jerusalem, rebuke you! Is this not a brand plucked from the fire?" Now Jeshua was clothed with filthy garments and standing before the angel. He spoke and said to those who were standing before him, saying, "Remove the filthy garments from him". Again he said to him, "See, I have taken your iniquity away from you and will clothe you with festal robes."*

Then I said, "Let them put a clean turban on his head." So they put a clean turban on his head and clothed him with garments, while the angel of the Lord was standing by. And the angel of the Lord admonished Jeshua, saying, "Thus says the Lord of hosts, 'If you will walk in My ways and if you will perform My service, then you will also govern My house and also have charge of My courts, and I will grant you free access among these who are standing here'" (Zechariah 4:1-5).

Fabulous revelation of love—in Heaven, God rebukes satan, declares Jeshua justified, and promises him access to His courts if he walks in God's ways.

2. Zechariah also had a word for Zerubbabel. It contains a verse that is familiar to many but this context gives it added meaning.

This is the word of the Lord to Zerubbabel saying, "Not by might nor by power, but by My Spirit," says the Lord of hosts. "What are you, O great mountain? Before Zerubbabel you will become a plain; and he will bring forth the top stone with shouts of 'Grace, grace to it!'" Also the word of the Lord came to me, saying, "The hands of Zerubbabel have laid the foundation of this house, and his hands will finish it. Then you will know that the Lord of hosts has sent me to you for who has despised the day of small things?" (Zechariah 4:6-10).

God declares the victory over Zerubbabel's opposition through His Spirit and proclaims that Zerubbabel will finish building the Temple. What a powerful, inspirational word to this man of God who was under attack by the enemy, discouraged, and worn by years of labor.

STAGE TWO REVIVAL (GOD RETURNS TO HIS PEOPLE)

Some of the Lord's enemies objected to the resumption of work and appealed to the king of Persia. This time, however, the outcome was far different than it had been 15 years earlier. God's favor was with Israel—they had not only returned to Jerusalem, they had returned to the Lord. The Persian king commanded work to continue and even issued an edict that those who had been opposing the building project would have to pay the cost of construction (see Ezra 5:3-6:10). It was **a miraculous intervention** by the Lord (Result #1). A new infusion of power and grace flooded Jerusalem and the Temple was completed. God gave much credit for the final success to the prophets that supported the leaders. May prophets arise in our day to encourage the brethren (see Ezra 6:14).

The people of Jerusalem celebrated the dedication of the House of God with **joy** (Result #3) (Ezra 6:16). If we build up the House of the Lord as a place of worship, we will have joy as well. They **offered sacrifice** (Result #7). The offering for the dedication of the Temple was 100 bulls, 200 rams, and 400 lambs. They also made a sin offering, *"twelve male goats, corresponding to the number of the tribes of Israel"* (Ezra 6:17).

Ministry was organized (Result #6) in the temple according to the Word (Ezra 6:18). It is interesting to note that they made a sin offering for all 12 tribes. We remember that it was primarily the tribes of Benjamin and Judah who responded and made the arduous journey back to Jerusalem. They were the ones who faced the pressure and the trials. They were the ones who did the hard work of completing the building. Most would say that they should have been the only ones to enjoy the building. But we aren't talking about just any house here. This was God's House; it was restored for all of God's children. *It is for all those who know the Lord, and it is for all those who don't know the Lord...yet!* May the "lost" tribes come to the Lord's House.

REVIVAL THEME

Zerubbabel and Jeshua were intent on rebuilding the Temple of the Lord. There is a parallel between rebuilding the Temple and revival. Revival can be seen as reconstructing a body of believers in such a way that the Lord will choose to dwell within them in divine fire and glory. Wherever, and for whatever reason, we have allowed the Church to fall into disrepair; it must be built up again. The work of the Lord may seem to have been destroyed in certain places and the saints languish in spiritual captivity. Nevertheless, the Lord has rebuilding in mind.

ENDNOTE

1.   A narrative based on Ezra 1-6 and Luke 2:25-32.

POINTS TO PONDER

1. The people in Babylon were offered the opportunity to move to Jerusalem—God's place—and rebuild the Temple, God's plan. We too, are offered that same challenge on a spiritual plane. We can return to God and build up a spiritual house of worship. How will you move toward God and into His plan?

2. There was a lot of opposition to rebuilding the Temple in Jerusalem. It took a huge commitment of time, energy, and finances. Are you committed to working together with others to build up the house of the Lord in spite of opposition? How do you demonstrate this?

3. Opposition halted the rebuilding of the Temple after the foundation had been laid. How does this speak to us about Christ's work on the Cross and what remains to be done?

4. Haggai 2:1-9 reveals that though smaller and less ornate than Solomon's Temple, Zerubbabel's Temple was destined to have greater glory. What is meant by this?

Chapter 12

The Ezra Revival
Separation from the World

Repentance in the Rain[1]

It was midday in Jerusalem as a group of priests and Levites conferred in the Temple court. Some had recently arrived from Babylon. Among them was Ezra, a priest and scribe, the leader of the new arrivals. A startled, almost terrified look came over his strong and handsome features as he listened to a report on the current situation in Israel. Ezra was stunned to the point of paralysis for a moment by the news he heard. He had expected everything to be in order in Jerusalem. After all, it was God's city. He tried to speak...his lips moved, but uttered no sound. Finally, a wail escaped as he pulled violently at his curly hair and beard. *Tendrils of brown hair, ripped from their roots, clung to his fingers as he collapsed, appalled.* He then ripped the tunic he wore from the collar to the waistband. Grasping his long robe in both hands, he tore it, too. Not satisfied, he scooped handfuls of dust into the air—most of it settling on him—and continued to wail.

The news that shocked Ezra was that many Israelites had intermarried with Canaanites from the surrounding territories. Making matters worse, the priests and Levites had reported that a large number of Jerusalem's spiritual leaders were involved in this serious breach of God's law.

Ezra had come to Jerusalem excited to be in the land of Israel; now he was devastated. Skilled in God's Word, he knew that the Lord's plans to restore the nation and fulfill His will were in jeopardy. This priest was certain that if Israel persisted in ignoring God's precepts, captivity and eventual destruction would follow. Ezra's sorrow for sin and spiritual rebellion was a catalyst that galvanized others there to kneel and pray as well. Conviction even flowed over some in the gathering who were offenders. Grief and outrage pressed down on the group praying in the court of the Temple.

By word of mouth, news spread that something was happening at the Temple. People began to congregate at the entrance to the court. Many quietly and solemnly filtered in to the court sensing the holy atmosphere. Waning daylight found a growing assembly seeking the Lord. Ezra, hands stretched out, was on his knees, rocking slightly in silent prayer. Tears had made trails on his dusty cheeks. He wept again as he prayed aloud:

O my God, I am ashamed and embarrassed to lift up my face to You, for our iniquities have risen above our heads and our guilt has grown even to the heavens. Because of our sins we fell to the

*sword and captivity and open shame. And now we are doing it
again, O God!* (Ezra 9:6-7)

Ezra's study and love of the Word made him sensitive to
how dangerous this situation had become.

*You have shown us grace. A remnant has returned to the land
and You have given us a peg in this holy place. You extended lovingkindness to us in the sight of kings, to raise up the house of
our God and to restore the ruins in Judah and Jerusalem* (Ezra
9:8-9).

Ezra stretched out on the ground, his face pressed against
the cool stone pavement.

*Now, O Lord, what can we say? We have forsaken Your command-
ments* [again]. *You said, "The land which you are entering to possess is an unclean land…filled with…abominations from end
to end. Do not give your daughters to their sons nor take their
daughters to your sons* [lest you learn to do as they do]" (Ezra
9:10-12).

The tears started to flow again as Ezra agonized, oblivious
to the purple shadows lengthening in the square. A heavy
presence hung, almost palpable, in the air.

The sun set behind the Temple. A throng of people now
filled most of the court. The scribe continued to lift his
voice, fervency in his words, *"You have punished us less than
our iniquities deserve, and have given us an escaped remnant"*
(Ezra. 9:13). As Ezra prayed, many people were also

weeping. Some were prostrate on the ground, like Ezra. Others knelt, thousands stood silently in prayer. Ezra continued:

Shall we again break Your commandments and intermarry with the peoples who commit these abominations? Would You not be angry with us to the point of destruction, until there is no remnant nor any who escape? O Lord God of Israel, You are righteous. We are before You in our guilt, for no one can stand before You because of this (Ezra 9:14-15).

In the outer court, a group of children were on their knees crying out, seeking the Lord's mercy. Women's voices moaned and softly wailed in distress. Quiet slowly began to envelop Jerusalem that night, but no one wanted to return to their homes.

It was then that Shecaniah the son of Jehiel stood and spoke; his voice carried across the crowd.

We have been unfaithful to our God and have married foreign women from the peoples of the land; yet now there is hope for Israel in spite of this. So now let us make a covenant with our God to put away all the wives and their children, according to the counsel of my lord,

He then gestured to Ezra and the group of priests:

and of those who tremble at the commandment of our God; and let it be done according to the law (Ezra 10:2-3).

Murmurs of agreement began to reverberate throughout the Temple court. Ezra lifted his eyes and saw moonlight reflected on thousands of faces looking to him. Shecaniah came near to him, leaned over the stricken priest and spoke softly, *"Ezra, get up. You must show us what to do. This matter is your responsibility, but we will be with you; be courageous and act. We will do as you say"* (see Ezra 10:4). Ezra slowly rose from the ground, straightened his torn robe, and looked at the other priests and Levites who were near, and again scanned the crowd. Muscles worked in his jaw, and his voice was intense as he asked loudly, "Will you do as I say?" All who were there nodded and swore they would, murmuring their amens. Ezra walked slowly toward the Temple proper. Stopping at the door he turned and said sadly, **"Bring all Israel to assemble before the Lord in three days time."** He made his way into the Temple to stay in the chamber of Jehohanan.

Three days later, the people of Jerusalem and the surrounding environs sat in the open square before the House of God. A heavy rain fell from low murky clouds, soaking everyone. But no one left the court. Many shivered and trembled, not only because of the rain, but also because of the agony they knew lay ahead. Ezra stood in the center of the large gathering, water running in rivulets from his hair and beard. His clothing was soaked. He had neither eaten nor drunk in three days, mourning over the sin of Israel. He gritted his teeth and steeled himself, not against the storm but against the sorrow and pain he knew his words would bring. The pain was of the people's own making; nevertheless, his heart ached and his voice broke in deeply felt emotion as he shouted above the downpour so all could hear.

You have been unfaithful...adding to the guilt of Israel. Now therefore, make confession to the Lord God of your fathers and do His will; separate yourselves from the peoples of the land and from your foreign wives! (Ezra 10:10-11)

The people of Jerusalem had vowed obedience. Still, Ezra wondered how they would respond. But something had happened in their hearts that night as they lay weeping before God. They had made a decision—they would be the people of the Lord! With a loud voice, the crowd spoke almost as one, *"As you have said, so it is our duty to do. Let the fierce anger of our God on account of this matter be turned away from us"* (see Ezra. 10:12,14). Teardrops mingled with raindrops on their faces as they rose to obey.

THE SETTING FOR REVIVAL

The Temple had been rebuilt 60 years earlier. Despite that past spiritual victory, it was now evident that things were not right in Jerusalem. Much of the city still lay in devastation and the people of Israel were still unwilling to be separate, holy people. Many of them had taken wives from the Canaanite peoples. Ezra understood the peril this callous disregard of God's commands placed Israel in. He knew their destiny as a nation and as a people was at stake. This is illustrative of the Church today; many seem to think we can live like the world—intermarrying with its perverted values and godless self-addiction—without suffering loss. Like Israel, we must turn from our disobedience and return to the Lord though the cost may be high to do so.

STAGE ONE REVIVAL (GOD'S PEOPLE RETURN TO HIM)

A strong godly leader arose (Component #1). Ezra was descended from Aaron through Zadok. The Bible says, *"The good hand of God was upon him"* (Ezra 7:9). Saying God's hand is on you is a way of expressing you have favor from the Lord. In Scripture, God's hand is credited with blessings, protection, and guidance. The strong godly leader has God's gracious hand on his life because, like Ezra, he sets *"his heart to study the law of the Lord, to practice it, and to teach His statutes and ordinances"* (Ezra 7:10).

The Church, for the most part, has not set its heart on the Word. Bible study attendance in the average church is much smaller than attendance at a worship service. People often chafe at substantive times of preaching and teaching, even on Sunday morning, "A 20-minute sermon is all we need, pastor." **If the Bible is food for the soul, many Christians are on a starvation diet.**

Ezra knew that acquiring a full understanding of the Word of God required diligent study. May the Lord give us passion enough to say we are not satisfied with a morsel of the Word of God. May we devote ourselves to study, motivated to grasp the whole of it.

Ezra also set his heart to practice the Word. He not only talked the talk, he walked the walk. He wanted to gain knowledge of the Word of God, but he also longed to put it into practice in order to habitually exercise God's will in his life. Today, Christianity often seems to be less a matter of commitment and more a matter of convenience. Following Christ and maintaining a relationship with Him will not always be convenient. In contrast to this unfortunate trend, Ezra demonstrated radical conformity to the Word of God.

The priest was also committed to teach God's Word. Those who know and grow in the Word of God are not satisfied with simply knowing the truth themselves—or even personally practicing its precepts. Like Ezra, they want to communicate the wonderful revelation to others. This is the natural and correct result of a personal commitment to truth—you have to share it with someone!

When the group returning to Jerusalem with Ezra assembled in preparation for the trip (Ezra 7:15), **Ezra proclaimed a fast** (Component #17). The fast was a way of humbling themselves before God and seeking a safe journey (Ezra 7:21). After three days, they broke camp and **moved** (Component #20) back to the land of Israel. This group returning from captivity is to be commended. They had been born and raised in Babylon. Launching out on a long journey in dangerous times took courage. This fear may be why some people are always talking about getting back to God, but never find the time or energy needed to actually do so.

The Israelites arrived safely in Jerusalem (see Ezra 7:31-32). The first thing they did upon arriving was **offer sacrifices** (Component #10) to the Lord (see Ezra 7:33). While this was a good start, Ezra soon found there was a major problem in the city. Many of the people, including Jerusalem's leaders, had joined in marriage with women from the surrounding Canaanite nations. Captivity had come to Israel just a few generations before because of the idolatry and corruption caused by this very thing.

Ezra was aghast and deeply grieved. As a true spiritual leader, he owned responsibility for the sins of his people. Their sin made him fall before God in shame. The tearing of his garments speaks of mourning. He humbly labored in intercessory prayer for hours in God's presence, stretching out his hands to the Lord. He thanked God for grace, grateful that He had not forsaken them despite their sin. Ezra acknowledged that they had no excuse and that their position before the Lord was tenuous. **He understood, and expressed, that except for an outpouring of mercy, they were all doomed** (see Ezra 9:6-15). Should we not also have this heart today?

Others saw the intensity of Ezra's sorrow and joined him (see Ezra 9:3-4). They began to **pray together** (Component #7). A very large assembly—men, women, and children—eventually gathered to Ezra. The intensity and passion of a strong godly leader will be communicated to those around him. This is what triggers the fundamental realignment of affection and obedience to God in stage one revival.

As the nation lay under conviction in the great court of the Temple, Shecaniah said to Ezra, "We have been unfaithful to our God and have married foreign women from the peoples of the land...yet now there is hope for Israel in spite of this." Thank God for Shecaniah! He came to Ezra and made an appeal on behalf of the people:

> Let us make a covenant with our God to put away all the wives
> and their children, according to the counsel of my lord and of
> those who tremble at the commandment of our God; and let it be
> done according to the law (Ezra 10:3).

What an awesome turn of events. The survivors of God's earlier judgment on Judah were willing to do whatever was necessary to return to Him. This was, and is, the sign of true repentance.

Some nonbelievers point out that Christians and churches are imperfect and often dysfunctional. Such critics are correct, for, like Israel, the Church easily and repeatedly entangles itself with worldly values and practices. It is a major problem and hindrance to revival.

But the people joined in **a shared vision** (Component #2) of disengaging from the world and living for the Lord (Ezra 10:4). They changed their way of thinking and **committed to obey God's Word** (Component #3) (Ezra 10:3).

The nation **gathered in unity** (Component #4) when a proclamation was made to come to Jerusalem. Failure to appear would mean exclusion from the commonwealth and forfeiture of possessions (see Ezra 10:7-8). They assembled on the appointed day, **demonstrating obedience to human authority** (Component #12). They sat trembling in the Temple court because of the rain and the difficult decision many of them faced. But they knew what must be done (see Ezra 10:9-10). Ezra called them to **separate from the world** (Component #11) by putting away their Canaanite wives and children (see Ezra 10:12-44).

The dissolution of families that took place under Ezra's leadership may sound extreme, but we have to remember what was at stake—not only the survival of the nation, but the survival of God's plan of salvation. What Israel did then is no excuse to divorce unbelieving spouses today. As Christians, we are not to be "unequally yoked" by marrying unbelievers. Yet, First Corinthians 7 instructs Christians not to divorce an unbelieving spouse, if already married.

The **repentance** (Component #12) that swept over the people was intense and genuine (see Ezra 10:1). True repentance is not expressed by a few quick words just to relieve some emotional or spiritual pain. A shallow "sorry" won't suffice when we have wandered far from the Lord. True repentance demands a change of heart and thinking, backed up by a change of behavior in spite of great cost.

While there is no reported stage two to this revival, it was still a deep renewal of spiritual life. We may consider the calamity that, in all certainty, would have occurred without this corrective return to God, not to mention the preservation of the nation until the coming of Messiah. Ezra's revival also set the stage for Nehemiah's spiritual and political leadership. Nehemiah's arrival in Jerusalem 20 years later would spark the last great revival in the Old Testament.

REVIVAL THEME

Ezra's revival brings home a vital and challenging truth. The Church must separate from the ways of the world. An intermarriage of the kingdom of truth and light with the kingdom of falsehood and darkness will never stand in God's sight. Our energy, power, and blessings are sapped when we compromise God's standards of purity.

ENDNOTE

1.   A narrative based on Ezra 9 and 10.

Points to Ponder

1. Ezra found there was a major problem in the city of Jerusalem. Many of the people had married people from the surrounding Canaanite nations. Does this have a spiritual parallel in the Church today?

2. Ezra understood the peril this practice of intermarriage placed Israel in. He knew their destiny was at stake. What price did Israel pay? What consequences confront the Church from intermarriage with the world?

3. What are some of the things that the Church intermarries with?

4. What are some of the children (results) of this intermarriage?

5. Israel was willing to do whatever was necessary to return to God. It was, and is, the sign of true repentance. What was it that brought Israel to the place of repentance?

Chapter 13

The Nehemiah Revival
Rebuilding Christian Character

The Wall[1]

The man walking atop Jerusalem's wall was well dressed; his clothing and shoes spoke of wealth and privilege. The middle-aged features of his face were stern but somehow softened by his eyes. He moved with a strong and elegant stride refined by years in a king's court. At his request, Nehemiah had recently been appointed governor of Jerusalem by Artaxerxes, ruler of the Persian Empire.

The walkway on top of the wall was wide and offered plenty of room for the governor's stroll. As he reached the Sheep Gate, he again enjoyed his favorite view of the Temple and the city. The setting sun bathed everything in a rosy glow. Nehemiah's eyes followed the now complete circle of the wall around the city. He thought, "Even my enemies acknowledge it is miraculous to have completed it so quickly."

Rebuilding the wall had been a monumental project. Nehemiah was amazed at the achievement himself. He took a deep breath, let it out slowly and relaxed—really relaxed—for the first time in several months. For long minutes, while the sky darkened, he just stood and savored the scene. Peace and a sense of security were finally realities in the city of David. As Nehemiah continued along the wall, he couldn't help inspecting the workmanship again. He was pleased that the large stones had been well and truly set, even though most of the work had not been done by masons. The wall was put together with what was available—by those who were willing to work. Many of the stones had been broken in the cataclysmic fall of Jerusalem 150 years before. Some were still black from fire that had swept the city. But now, the breaches had been carefully built up. "The gates stand and the wall is strong," Nehemiah thought with deep satisfaction.

The next day, Nehemiah and all Israel would dedicate the gates and walls of Jerusalem to the Lord. Levitical singers from all the cities and villages of Judah were already in the city. Nehemiah could hear the singers practicing their songs in the soft warm twilight; the city was filled with praise rising from hundreds of voices. Earlier in the day, the priests and Levites had consecrated themselves and the people. The rising moon found the governor still on the wall, weeping joyful tears and kneeling in prayer over the city he loved.

Morning dawned in spectacular beauty, as if the heavens were celebrating the accomplishment of God's people. Bright sunshine found the denizens of the city in the court of the Temple—except for the Levites, leaders, and a large contingent of musicians and singers who were assembled at the eastern gate. The gathering at the gate split into two groups, each led by a powerful choir and orchestra. Ezra the scribe and one group went to the right. They proceeded along the base of the wall with joyful singing. At the Fountain Gate they climbed the stairway of the wall to the Water Gate on the east and proceeded toward the Temple. Nehemiah and the other group followed the second choir to the left. Walking along the top of the wall, they made their way past the tower of furnaces, the Old Gate, and the Tower of Hananel. They would meet the others at the House of the Lord.

When they arrived at the Temple, the two great choirs took their stand at opposite ends of the court. At first, they sang responsively, the harmonies and interplay of song and music swelling and enthralling the listeners. Trumpets sounded and the singers merged into one combined choir. They lifted songs of praise in unison to the Lord. Everyone worshiped as a God-given joy permeated the crowd. Men, women, and children joyfully shouted. After many years of shame and vulnerability to attack, Jerusalem stood strong again.

THE SETTING FOR REVIVAL

Eighty years before Nehemiah's appointment as governor of Jerusalem a group of almost 50,000 captives returned to the city from Babylon. Led by Zerubbabel and Jeshua, they rebuilt the Temple. Sixty years later, a godly priest named Ezra led another group home. Under his leadership, some things were set straight, but there was still great need in Jerusalem. The wall of the city had been demolished by the conquering Babylonians and the city remained defenseless and in shambles.

STAGE ONE REVIVAL (GOD'S PEOPLE RETURN TO HIM)

In 444 B.C., 20 years after Ezra's group returned, God found a man who would lead the reconstruction of the city wall. That man was Nehemiah. Under his **strong godly leadership** (Component #1), revival would come again to Jerusalem. Nehemiah lived in Persia's capital city and served in the king's court. He became aware of the situation in Jerusalem when his brother, Hananiah, came to visit him. Nehemiah asked how everything was going in Judah. Hananiah's answer was disturbing:

> *The remnant there who survived the captivity is in great distress and reproach. The people are robbed, harassed and even killed and the wall of Jerusalem is broken down and its gates are burned with fire* (Nehemiah 1:3).

Nehemiah lived hundreds of miles away from Jerusalem. To do anything would be costly and would upset his comfortable life. He had a prominent and important job. As long as he didn't lose the king's favor, he was "set for life," but Nehemiah had a genuine concern for the Lord's people and the city of Jerusalem.

Nehemiah responded first in prayer, *"When I heard these things…I sat down…and I prayed before the God of heaven"* (Neh. 1:3). I appreciate that Nehemiah didn't just give advice to his brother. He didn't offer to speak to the king about the situation. He didn't sit down and write a check to try and fix the problem. I appreciate what he *did* do: he humbled himself before the God of Heaven and prayed. Here is a man who has been confronted with a huge problem. He feels an intense burden, but he does nothing—he goes nowhere until he fervently prays about it. Too often we are quick to offer answers, attempt a rash solution, or simply grieve over bad news.

Bad news of the magnitude Hananiah reported should bring us to the place of deep prayer. Nehemiah entered a season of serious prayer and he prayed with passion. *"When I heard these things, I...wept. For some days I mourned"* (Neh. 1:4). Nehemiah allowed himself to be touched emotionally. He deliberately entered into the problem and was brokenhearted. Nothing superficial characterized his response.

Hananiah's description of Jerusalem in disarray and danger is an analogy of the backslidden church. There is "great distress and reproach," the people are spiritually "robbed, harassed, and even killed." This accurately describes the Church desperately needing to return to God. If a report of weakness and vulnerability in the Church comes to us, will we sit down and fervently pray or will we be apathetic? When the Church is harassed and weak— when things are not right among God's people—it should break our hearts, as it did Nehemiah's. Will we just continue living our lives and paying the bills? Or will we respond when God is looking for someone who will rebuild?

Nehemiah **confessed sin on behalf of the nation** (Component #13) and appealed to the covenant-keeper God:

> *I beseech You...let Your ear now be attentive and Your eyes open to hear the prayer of Your servant which I am praying before You now, day and night, on behalf of the sons of Israel Your servants, confessing the sins of the sons of Israel which we have sinned against You; I and my father's house have sinned* (Nehemiah 1:5-6).

He appealed to God's promise of mercy:

> *Remember the word which You did command Your servant Moses, saying, "If you are unfaithful I will scatter you among the peoples;*

but if you return to Me and keep My commandments and do them, though those of you who have been scattered were in the most remote part of the heavens, I will gather them from there and will bring them to the place where I have chosen to cause My name to dwell"(Nehemiah 1:8-9).

Nehemiah supercharged his prayers with the discipline of fasting (Component #17) (see Neh. 1:4). His prayer and fasting for the situation was sustained over a four-month period (see Neh. 1:5-11). Like Nehemiah, we must persevere in prayer. At the end of the four months, his request to go to Jerusalem found favor with the king (see Neh. 2:5).

Nehemiah accepted his destiny and embraced the vision of rebuilding the city of God. When Nehemiah first arrived in Jerusalem, his first action was to survey the situation at night. That night, he realized that rebuilding the wall was obviously going to be a huge and difficult task (see Neh. 2:12). I admire Nehemiah. Though the situation was daunting, he was determined! It was a big job, but we've got a big God! He refused to say, "It's hopeless and I'm helpless." Instead, he said, *"The hand of the Lord is on me. We're going to build"* (Neh. 2:18).

At first there were only a few individuals who shared his vision of rebuilding the wall (see Neh. 2:12). This is often the way revival starts; a few brave individuals see the need and accept the burden with faith and determination. After surveying the wall, Nehemiah addressed the population of Jerusalem, *"You see the bad situation we are in, that Jerusalem is desolate and its gates burned by fire. Come; let us rebuild the wall of Jerusalem so that we will no longer be a reproach."* He also told them how God had been with him and about the king's promise of support. Nehemiah established a link between what God was doing through him and demonstrated that God had been working behind the scenes for their benefit. It awakened the people's dormant faith and they boldly responded, *"Let us arise and build."* It is exciting when people **share the vision** (Component #2) (Neh. 2:17-18).

It is important to understand that the walls of Jerusalem represent Christian character in our personal lives, families, and churches. When our character is broken down, we become a reproach to the Lord and vulnerable to attack. While our strength is in the Lord, strong character provides some spiritual protection. Rebuilding the wall means reordering our ways to live with Spirit-born integrity, compassion, and self-control. In short, the wall is about conducting our lives in accordance with God's standards.

The Church is like a city; its walls of righteous character can be broken down. The sad thing is that the backslidden church often has not had an enemy invade and break down the walls by force. Christians often dismantle the walls of character themselves so that they can be "free." Many don't understand the danger in doing so. We become vulnerable. With our protective walls broken down, the enemy of our souls continues to steal, kill, and destroy. *If you live in a place with no walls everything gets in and nothing stays out*; nothing slows the intrusions of the world. Worst of all, the absence of the protective wall around Jerusalem meant the Temple was vulnerable to attack. The Temple represents worship and the presence of God. Is the place where God resides in your heart protected by the "walls" of strong character? Is the church where you worship strengthened by men and women of godly character?

Thankfully, God cares about us and longs to lead us in rebuilding character in our lives. Nehemiah's name means "the comfort of God." This is a picture of the One identified by Jesus as The Comforter. Great distress and reproach may abound in your life but you are not without hope! God has sent the Holy Spirit.

Led by Nehemiah, **the inhabitants of Jerusalem began to build** (Component #16). *"They put their hands to the good work"* (Neh. 2:18). If we want to see revival in our lives, if we want to see distress and reproach removed, then we must work. The work on the wall was accomplished shoulder to shoulder. Note the variety of backgrounds of those who worked to rebuild the wall: priests, goldsmiths, perfume-makers, merchants, and district rulers. Also note Nehemiah 3:12, *"Next to (Hashub) Shallum the son of Hallohesh...repaired, he and his daughters."* This rebuilding effort was not exclusively men's work. It was for all who had a stake in the critically important project of rebuilding the wall.

This sense of **unity** (Component #4) is a lesson we continually need to learn and encourage in the Church. We will never move beyond how well we are getting along. If we are not united by a biblical purpose, we will nit-pick, gossip, and argue, while failing to accomplish God's agenda. We must have the courage to become team players. The Lord has called us to engage in coordinated cooperation. He calls us to have the courage to set aside our preferences, our desires, our hurts, and our pride for the sake of success. Nehemiah took a disorganized, unmotivated, and uninspired group and turned them into an army with a mission.

In Nehemiah 4:6, we read that they reached a milestone. *"We built the wall and the whole wall was joined together to half its height for the people had a mind to work."* Their unity of vision and labor began to produce results.

It would be nice if we only had to build, but we must battle as well. Significant progress in rebuilding the wall meant that Nehemiah and company were going to have to contend with opposition. An enemy coalition led by Sanballat, Tobiah, Geshem, together with hidden opposition inside the city desperately opposed Nehemiah. The kingdom of darkness consistently opposes revival. Winning without warfare is impossible. There is no opportunity without opposition, no victory without vigilance, and no testimony without a test.

It is imperative that we understand how to deal with **opposition** (Result #15). Nehemiah faced and overcame his opposition in order to complete his mission. We can learn much from his example. The enemy used four major strategies against Nehemiah and his team:

1. **Verbal assaults on the laborers**

   Tobiah and his cronies mocked the work (Neh. 2:19-20, 4:1-3). The result was demoralization of Nehemiah's workers (see Neh. 4:5).

   Nehemiah's response to this attack was **united prayer** (see Neh. 4:4) (Component #7) and a determination to keep working (see Neh. 4:6). Notice the two-pronged solution—prayer and perspiration. The believer must continue in prayer and be stubborn about completing the work assigned by God.

2. **"Disturbances" in the city**

   Nehemiah's opponents discovered their initial insults did not stop the builders. This so infuriated Tobiah and company they conspired to cause "disturbances" in the city (see Neh. 4:8). Nehemiah's response to the new attack again had two components:

   - Prayer: *"We prayed to our God"* (Neh. 4:9).

   - Vigilance: *"We set up a guard against them day and night"* (Neh. 4:9).

     Notice the continued unity—"*We* prayed.... *We* set up a guard." The people of God were in this work together. While the nature of these "disturbances" is not explained, it is apparent by the posting of guards that Nehemiah's opponents fomented some sort of demonstration or vandalism within the city.

3. **Threats of violence and murder**

   The attacks continued to escalate in the form of terrorism. Fear stalked the city (see Neh. 4:11-12,14). Nehemiah countered these menacing threats by encouraging the workers, *"Remember the Lord who is great and awesome"* (Neh.

4:13). He also exhorted them to recognize what was at stake, *"Fight for your brothers, your sons, for your daughters, for your wives, and for your houses"* (Neh. 4:14). He also strategically placed armed teams (see Neh. 4:19) and created a plan to rally to any point of attack (see Neh. 4:19-23). All the while, of course, they continued to labor on the wall (see Neh. 4:21).

For the rebuilders of Jerusalem, there was no backing off or slowing down. They were on a mission from God. Let us also recognize the enormity of the stakes and allow this realization to motivate us to the task of building our character in Christ. The goal of character building is neither for the half-hearted nor faint-hearted. Satan tries to scare us and make us quit. We must have the strength to withstand fear and attacks.

In the midst of these attacks, when harmony was sorely needed, strife arose among the Israelites themselves. Legitimate complaints began to surface. Some of the people said, "We're starving." When work on the wall began, people left their jobs, fields, and vineyards. This created major supply problems (see Neh. 5:1-2). Others were borrowing against the value of their homes to survive (Neh. 5:3). Still others complained, *"We're being enslaved because we have had to borrow money to pay the king's tax on our fields and vineyards"* (Neh. 5:4).

The answer was not to ignore the king's tax or to stop work on the wall. The problem was something else, and Nehemiah was genuinely angry about it (see Neh. 5:1-2). Many Jews had returned from captivity and gotten into "debt trouble" with their fellow Jews. They found themselves sold back into slavery through the practice of usury. Nehemiah reminded them all this practice of loaning money at interest was prohibited in God's Word, *"Do not take interest of any kind from him [your brother Israelite], but fear your God, so that your countryman may continue to live among you"* (Lev. 25:35-42). The way the people were treating each other revealed that they did not fear God. They had forgotten that only a few generations earlier they had been slaves with nothing to call their own, yet now they were enslaving others.

These problems were not technically an attack, although situations like these are often confused with outside opposition. They can be troubling and destructive to the work and they are often orchestrated and exploited by the enemy. These people were not objecting to the work; they were simply struggling to continue. In actuality, this was a spiritual problem among God's people, one that needed to be rectified immediately. Led by Nehemiah, **they repented of their wrong** (Component #12) and pledged, *"We will give it* (the money) *back and will require nothing from them; we will do exactly as you say"* (Neh. 5:12-13). God expects that the way we honor and care for each other will reveal the difference He has made in our lives. Jesus said, *"By this will all men know that you are my disciples, if you love one another"* (John 13:35).

4. A concerted and sustained attack on the strong godly leader

This virulent assault was a four-pronged onslaught:

- ### An attempt to isolate Nehemiah

The wall was nearing completion. It was finished except for the gates. Nehemiah's progress prompted Sanballat and Geshem to send a message to Nehemiah saying, *"Come, let us meet together"* (Neh. 6:1-2). The place of meeting was to be in a village on the plain of Ono, a little town right next to Samaria... Sanballat's home! Four times they invited Nehemiah into this trap. Nehemiah was sure they were scheming to harm him, so he sent his regrets. He said, in effect, "Oh, no!" to Ono.

When we are effective in ministry, satan often attempts to get us on our own—lonely and isolated. Close relationships with other believers frustrate the devil's plan. He will try to draw us out of fellowship and away from what we should be doing. Nehemiah sent messengers to his foes saying, *"I am doing a great work and I cannot come down. Why should the work stop while I leave it and come down to you?"* (Neh. 6:3-4).

• *Untruthful and unsubstantiated allegations*

When the plan to separate Nehemiah from his support and protection failed, his enemies created rumors that Nehemiah had ulterior motives—Sanballat sent an *open* letter to Jerusalem and Nehemiah:

It is reported among the nations, and Gashmu says, that you and the Jews are planning to rebel; therefore you are rebuilding the wall. And you are to be their king, according to these reports. You have also appointed prophets to proclaim in Jerusalem concerning you, "A king is in Judah!" And now it will be reported to the king [of Persia] according to these reports. So come now, let us take counsel together (Nehemiah 6:5-8).

This was a public relations ploy, calculated to fuel speculation and rumor. In addition, it was intended to make Nehemiah think that everyone was beginning to believe the worst about him. Sanballat was saying, "Nehemiah, everyone can see that this has gone to your head. You are going to declare yourself king and rebel against Artaxerxes, and we are going to tell the king on you!"

Nehemiah's foes also wanted to create uncertainty and fear in the people. If the assertion was true that Nehemiah was planning to rebel, the full force of the Persian Empire would crush them.

This type of attack against leadership forces us to realize that the truth is not always going to be told. God's enemies questioned Nehemiah's character and his motives. Tragically, this tactic often works. Many people have experienced disappointment and betrayal at the hand of leaders. Thus, they tend to believe rumors that are spread by those who try to destroy the Lord's work.

Every pastor understands how difficult it must have been for Nehemiah to hear such accusations. At great personal sacrifice he had traveled to Judah for the good of Jerusalem and had lived and led with integrity. Now he was accused of the very opposite. His response at this crucial point kept the work on track. First, Nehemiah simply prayed, *"Lord, strengthen my hands."* He was undoubtedly hurt and discouraged by the accusations, but he continued the work because he kept his eyes on God instead of on his emotions. Second, Nehemiah refused to be belittled, deflected, or embittered. He replied to his accusers with a simple message, *"Such things as you are saying have not been done, but you are inventing them in your own mind"* (Neh. 6:8).

Sanballat and his friends desperately desired to overthrow Nehemiah because he was an effective leader. When our lives and ministries make a difference in our churches and cities we will suffer accusation. When the unfair criticism comes, it is tempting to defend ourselves and expend a lot of emotional strength arguing our case. We must learn to let God defend us, allowing time and patience to do their work. False accusations will be seen for what they are, and those who have perpetrated them will be discredited.

- *A diabolical plan designed to trap Nehemiah in sin*

Nehemiah's enemies concocted a devious scheme. A false friend told Nehemiah that his life was in danger and that he should hide in the Temple (see Neh. 6:10).

Nehemiah didn't fall for this. He said, *"Should a man like me flee? And could one such as I go into the temple to save his life? I will not go in."* (Neh. 6:11). Nehemiah knew that he must not enter the Temple (see Num. 3:10). The House of God was not built to be a hiding place for governors. While the law did make provision for asylum in the Temple in certain circumstances (see Num. 35:6), Nehemiah realized Tobiah and Sanballat had hired this so-called friend to frighten him and tempt him to sin. Then they would have an evil report with which to reproach him (see Neh. 6:10-14).

We must not fall into sin caused by fear. Nehemiah's example is a good one for us. His focus was not on self-preservation, but on the task he had been given. God had not sent him to *start* a wall, but to *finish* one!

- *A plot to undermine Nehemiah's authority through disloyal members of the city leadership*

There were influential people in Jerusalem whose allegiance was to Tobiah rather than to Nehemiah and the Lord! *"In those days many letters went from the nobles of Judah to Tobiah, and Tobiah's letters came to them. For many in Judah were bound by oath to him... moreover, they were speaking about his good deeds in my presence and reported my words to him"* (Neh. 6:17-19).

We must not be surprised that some, even in church, will oppose the God-given leader and plan. Nehemiah's response was straight forward and focused: he kept working.

STAGE TWO REVIVAL (GOD RETURNS TO HIS PEOPLE)

A miracle occurred (Result #1). The wall was completed in 52 days. **This stupendous accomplishment intimidated Sanballat's coalition**: *"When all our enemies heard of it, and all the nations surrounding us saw it, they lost their confidence"* (Neh. 6:16). God was glorified. Everyone recognized that the work had been done with His help.

Peace came (Result #5). The enemy's harassment ceased and **ministry was set in order** (Result #6). With the city secure, Judah needed to become more organized in its temple worship. Gatekeepers, singers, and Levites were appointed (see Neh. 7:1-3).

At this point, Nehemiah could have sat back and basked in what they had accomplished, but rebuilding the wall was not an end in itself. He looked out across the city and noticed the city was large and spacious, but the people living in it were few (see Neh. 7:4). This is analogous to how many pastors feel on Sunday when they look out on their sanctuaries— great buildings built for the glory of God, and yet the inhabitants are few. It is good to have a house of worship, but in the final analysis, God is not interested in the dead stones of church buildings, but in the "living stones" of a spiritual house.

There was an outpouring of **giving to the Lord** (Result #8) (Neh. 7:70-72). And at the next national holiday the people **gathered "as one man"** (Component #4) in the square by the Water Gate (see Neh. 8:1). They asked Ezra to read the Book of the Law to the assembly. They were hungry to **hear the Word of God** (Components #3). They wanted to know how they could serve their great God. They certainly didn't come to be entertained or even to be comfortable. Ezra read from the Bible from early morning until midday, from daybreak till noon. For six hours they listened (see Neh. 8:3). When the Spirit of God is at work in revival, time becomes immaterial.

The Word was translated and explained by the scribes because many of these people no longer understood Hebrew (see Neh. 8:7-8). They had lived in Babylon so long they were totally ignorant of God's ways. (Similarly, for many people today the Bible is like a book written in a foreign language.) Everyone was attentive because of having experienced captivity; they wanted to hear the Word of liberty (see Neh. 8:3-4). They honored the Word by standing when Ezra opened the scrolls (see Neh. 8:5). Ezra blessed the Lord and the people answered, "Amen, Amen!" while lifting up their hands, then they bowed low and **worshiped the Lord** (Component #6) with their faces to the ground (see Neh. 8:6).

They were convicted by the Word, *"weeping when they heard the words of the law"*(Neh. 8:9). Nehemiah, Ezra, and the Levites said to them:

> *This day is holy to the Lord your God; do not mourn or weep. Go, eat of the fat, drink of the sweet, and send portions to him who has nothing prepared; for this day is holy to our Lord. Do not be grieved, for the joy of the Lord is your strength* (Nehemiah 8:10-12).

It was the Feast of Trumpets, commanded in Leviticus to be a day of rejoicing, so they rejoiced. Isn't it interesting that they didn't allow their emotions to govern their response to the Word. Rather, they ensured that obedience to the Word governed their emotions. They had been weeping, but now they began rejoicing. They did need a thorough time of repentance, and that would soon come. But this day was to be joyous.

The next day, the leaders of Judah came to Ezra again. They wanted more insight into the words of the Law (see Neh. 8:13-17). Here is a mighty work of God—and the test of any alleged revival in the Church—Does it bring the people closer to the Bible? Do they love it more? Does their respect for the truth of the Bible become greater, and do they obey its teaching more? Jesus said in John 17:17, *"Sanctify them by the truth.Your Word is truth."* God the Holy Spirit does His work in the environment of the Word of God. The people found that they couldn't do without the Word of God. Ezra read from the Book of the Law of God daily, from the first day to the last day of the seven day feast. And on the eighth day there was a solemn assembly (see Neh. 8:18).

Three and a half weeks later, something wonderful happened...on the twenty-fourth day of the month, the sons of Israel assembled again. This time they were fasting, wearing sackcloth, and covering themselves humbly in dirt. They **repented** (Component #12) at a deep level. The Word of God had done its work and brought conviction. They again stood in the Temple court and read from the Book of the Law. They confessed and **worshiped** (Component #6) the Lord. They separated themselves from all foreigners and **confessed their sins** and the iniquities of their fathers (Component #13) (see Neh. 9:1-3).

Nehemiah then led them in prayer (Component #7). He recounted God's merciful dealings with them (see Neh. 9:6-30). He ended his prayer with this appeal to God, found in Nehemiah 9:31-37:

> You did not make an end of [us] or forsake [us], forYou are a gra-
> cious and compassionate God. Now therefore, our God, the great,
> the mighty, and the awesome God, who keeps covenant and lov-
> ingkindness, Do not let all the hardship seem insignificant before
> You, which has come upon us, our kings, our princes, our priests,
> our prophets, our fathers and on allYour people, from the days of
> the kings of Assyria to this day. However,You are just in all that
> has come upon us; forYou have dealt faithfully, but we have acted
> wickedly. For our kings, our leaders, our priests and our fathers

have not kept Your law or paid attention to Your commandments and Your admonitions with which You have admonished them. But they, in their own kingdom, with Your great goodness which You gave them, with the broad and rich land which You set before them, did not serve You or turn from their evil deeds. Behold, we are slaves today, and as to the land which You gave to our fathers to eat of its fruit and its bounty, behold, we are slaves in it. Its abundant produce is for the kings whom You have set over us because of our sins; They also rule over our bodies and over our cattle as they please, so we are in great distress.

They made a serious covenant (Component #9) *"to walk in God's law"* (Neh. 10:28). The conditions of the covenant were as follows:

- They would **separate from the world** (Component #11)—they would no longer intermarry with those of other nations (see Neh. 10:30).

- They would keep the Sabbath and the Sabbatic year (see Neh. 10:31).

- **They would support God's House and God's men through tithes and offerings** (Component #8) (see Neh. 10:32; 12:44-45).

Additional **ministry was organized and raised up** (Result #7); notably, *"singers for the service of the house of God, for there was a commandment from the king concerning them and a firm regulation for the song leaders day by day"* (see Neh. 12:22-23).

Praise to God (Result #2) came forth as the walls of the city were dedicated. They sought out Levites and brought them to Jerusalem to celebrate the dedication with gladness (see Neh. 12:27). The priests and the Levites **purified** (or **consecrated**, Result #14) themselves, the people, the gates, and the wall (see Neh. 12:30). They rejoiced because God had given them **great joy** (Result #3) so that the joy of Jerusalem was heard from afar (see Neh. 12:43).

The revival almost ended prematurely. We are not told why, but Nehemiah went back to Babylon for a while. As noted earlier, Nehemiah represents the Holy Spirit. When the Holy Spirit is no longer in control, trouble will soon be. Nehemiah returned to Jerusalem to find the sanctity of the Temple had been compromised—Eliashib the priest, who was appointed over the chambers of the House of God, had prepared a large room for Tobiah to store his possessions. It turns out that Eliashib had been the inside man for Tobiah all the time; his son was married to one of Tobiah's daughters (see Neh. 13:28).

The room in question was of special importance to God-pleasing worship in the Temple. There, the grain offerings, the frankincense, the utensils and the tithes of grain, wine, and oil prescribed for the Levites, the singers and the gatekeepers, and the contributions for the priests were stored. A disastrous result had ensued—the Levites and singers had gone home because of a lack of support. In addition to these serious problems, the Sabbath was being broken again. And worst of all, they were *again* intermarrying with the people of the land! They had made an oath not to do these things, but they had not kept it (see Neh. 13:4-6). This illustrates the lukewarm believer compromising and allowing the world back into his life. Often the first things to be subverted are those things dedicated to ministry.

Thankfully, the revival was rescued. Nehemiah came back to Jerusalem and promptly threw all of Tobiah's goods out of the Temple. The room was cleansed and returned to God's use (see Neh. 13:7-9). Nehemiah restored the Levites to their posts and Judah resumed tithing on the grain, wine, and oil, bringing it into the Temple storehouses again. The Sabbath was reinstituted with a strong warning that was enforced. And the recurrent problem of mixed marriages was again dealt with (see Neh. 13:10-30).

The Holy Spirit continues to war against worldly inroads into our lives. We must be ever vigilant to maintain revival.

REVIVAL THEME

The revival led by Nehemiah reveals a great struggle centered on rebuilding Jerusalem's wall. The city wall represents Christian character in the Church. It is true that God is our strength and protector. However, we must learn to stand—to stand in righteousness. Continual and habitual sin opens us up to reproach, attack, and eventual defeat. In contrast, integrity and good character enable us to live in much greater safety and peace. True revival brings a rebuilding of fundamental values in the community of God.

ENDNOTE

1. A narrative based on Nehemiah 12:27-47.

POINTS TO PONDER

1. The remnant of people left in Jerusalem was in great distress and danger. Their situation illustrates a church in need of a return to God. Are you concerned about the state of your church?

2. The walls of Jerusalem represent Christian character in our personal lives, families, and churches. How does broken-down character leave us vulnerable to attack?

3. With no protective wall around Jerusalem, the Temple was in danger. What truth does this illustrate?

4. The enemies of Jerusalem became desperate to stop the rebuilding of the wall. What strategies did they use in their attacks?

THE POWER OF RETURN

"*Return to Me*." It is God's heart-cry. It is strong and emphatic. It is repeated and consistent. Whenever God's people wandered from Him, this clarion call, "*Return to Me*," was heard. It is both a command and a pleading request, one filled with promise and a proffered invitation to sweet reconciliation. It is an open door to a renewed relationship—all will be forgiven, just come back. Sometimes, it is so couched in the terms of a father's heartache that God's longing for His people is almost palpable. He commands a return. He pleads. He cajoles and is sometimes amazed that His people do not come back to Him.

Israel's future need for return to the Lord was prophetically described by Moses. Decades before their national apostasy (and generations before any Diaspora), Moses told of a time when the children of Israel would return to the Lord. Glimpsing the future, or maybe just so familiar with the character of God, Moses confidently proclaimed that when they returned, the people of God would find restoration and compassion.

> So it shall be when all of these things have come upon you, the blessing and the curse which I have set before you, and you call them to mind in all nations where the Lord your God has banished you, and you **return to the Lord** your God and obey Him

with all your heart and soul according to all that I command you today, you and your sons, then the Lord your God will restore you from captivity, and have compassion on you, and will gather you again from all the peoples where the Lord your God has scattered you (Deuteronomy 30:1-3).

"Return to the Lord!" This is the sage advice of all the prophets, from Moses to Malachi. Their words ring out across the centuries. Samuel, the last and mightiest of the judges, spoke to the whole house of Israel a thousand years before Christ, saying:

If you return to the Lord *with all your heart, remove the foreign gods and the Ashtaroth from among you and direct your hearts to the Lord and serve Him alone; He will deliver you from the hand of the Philistines* (1 Samuel 7:3).

It is a simple formula for victory: return, remove, direct, serve; and He will deliver you from the hand of your enemies!

With the exception of David, Hezekiah was the most commended king in Israel's history. At one point during his reign, he sent couriers throughout all Israel and Judah with letters from his hand saying, *"O sons of Israel,* **return to the Lord God** *of Abraham, Isaac and Israel,* **that He may return** *to those of you who escaped and are left from the hand of the kings of Assyria"* (2 Chron. 30:6). Hezekiah added:

*...***if you return to the Lord***, your brothers and your sons will find compassion before those who led them captive and will return to this land for the Lord your God is gracious and compassionate, and will not turn His face away from you ***if you return to Him*** (2 Chronicles 30:9).

Hosea spoke tenderly to Israel in the eighth century B.C., **"Come, let us return to the Lord** *for He has torn us, but He will heal us; He has wounded us, but He will bandage us"* (Hos. 6:1). Hosea was specific about how Israel's return should be accomplished: **"Take words with you and return to the Lord.** Say to Him, *"Take away all iniquity and receive us graciously that we may present the fruit of our lips"* (Hos. 14:2). Sadly, Israel did not listen, and God himself announced the results of nonreturn to Him. *"They will not return to the land of Egypt; but Assyria—he will be their king because **they refused to return to Me"*** (Hos. 11:5).

Isaiah, the king of the Old Testament prophets, spoke to Judah at about the same time. Early in his book (referenced by Jesus in Matt. 13:15), Isaiah recorded this sad and somewhat sarcastic command from the Lord:

> *Go, and tell this people: 'Keep on listening, but do not perceive; keep on looking, but do not understand.' Render the hearts of this people insensitive, their ears dull, and their eyes dim, otherwise they might see with their eyes, hear with their ears, understand with their hearts, **and return and be healed*** (Isaiah 6:9-10).

It is a commentary on those who continually hear the call but never come back to Him. Despite this grim observation, Isaiah's magnificent work still contains gracious encouragements to return:

- **Return to Him** *from whom you have deeply defected, O sons of Israel* (Isaiah 31:6).

- *Let the wicked forsake his way and the unrighteous man his thoughts; and **let him return to the Lord**, and He will have compassion on him, and to our God, for He will abundantly pardon* (Isaiah 55:7).

- In Isaiah 44:22 God Himself offers this invitation to return, *"I have wiped out your transgressions like a thick cloud, and your sins like a heavy mist.* **Return to Me,** *for I have redeemed you."*We need not fear judgment if we return before it is too late.

Jeremiah, the weeping prophet, expressed God's pain caused by the failure of Israel and Judah to return to Him even after they experienced much difficulty, trials, and grace.

- The Lord said, *"I thought, 'After she* [Israel] *has done all these things* **she will return to Me;'** *but she did not return"* (Jer. 3:7).

- After Israel's apostasy and destruction God was shocked that Judah did not run back to Him in sincerity. *"Yet in spite of all this her treacherous sister* **Judah did not return to Me with all her heart,** *but rather in deception"* (Jer. 3:10).

- Still, the Lord longed for them to make a steadfast decision to repent:

  > **"If you will return,** *O Israel," declares the Lord,* **"Then you should return to Me."***And if you will put away your detested things from My presence, and will not waver, and you will swear, 'As the Lord lives,' in truth, in justice and in righteousness; then the nations will bless themselves in Him, and in Him they will glory"* (Jeremiah 4:1-2).

  This offer included a revelation of "the power of return." Jeremiah promised that the nations will find the blessing and glory of the Lord if only God's people will return to Him.

- Before we leave Jeremiah we must note the wonderful prophesy in Chapter 24 verse 7: *"I will give them a heart to know Me, for I am the Lord; and they will be My people, and I will be their God, for* **they will return to Me with their whole heart."**

- Jeremiah finishes with this exhortation to everyone, *"Let us examine and probe our ways, and* **let us return to the Lord***"* (Lam. 3:40).

Zechariah, one of the prophets of a return to the Lord in the sixth century B.C., records the Lord's plea to that generation:

> *...Thus says the Lord of hosts,* **"Return to Me,"** *declares the Lord of hosts, 'that I may return to you.'*

God repeatedly identified himself as the one making this encouraging invitation as if to say, "It really is me saying this. I want you back (Zechariah 1:3).

There is a further exhortation in the next verse:

> *Do not be like your fathers, to whom the former prophets proclaimed, saying, "Thus says the Lord of hosts, '***Return now from your evil ways and from your evil deeds***. But they did not listen or give heed to Me...'"*(Zechariah 1:4).

The Lord's heart-cry 20 years later, voiced through Joel, is even more poignant.

> *"Yet even now," declares the Lord, "***Return to Me with all your heart***, and with fasting, weeping and mourning* (Joel 2:12).

Joel then echoes God's heart:

> *Rend your heart and not your garments.* **Now return to the Lord your God,** *for He is gracious and compassionate, slow to anger, abounding in lovingkindness and relenting of evil* (Joel 2:13).

The last prophet recorded in the Old Testament, Malachi, repeats the now familiar refrain.

> "From the days of your fathers you have turned aside from My statutes and have not kept them. **Return to Me, and I will return to you**," says the Lord of hosts (Malachi 3:7).

There were times that the children of Israel responded to the invitation and returned to the God of Abraham. When they did, they experienced His protection, provision, and presence. Yet when they did not respond, Israel's people suffered terrible consequences. The Church today faces the same choice. Though we live under a different covenant, we are as prone to wander as Israel was and often in need of heeding the call to return.

We must follow the path of "return" to have the power of His presence.

God, in His great wisdom, has given us the treasure of His Word. This repository of knowledge and revelation contains the answer for every dilemma and challenge we face, including the need for spiritual renewal of the local church. The fact that churches struggle with complacency, apathy, and backsliding certainly hasn't taken the Lord by surprise. He knew that Israel would wander, and He knows our wayward tendencies. Even so, His heart's cry and pleading invitation remain unchanged. He yearns for all to return to Him, including the lukewarm, backslidden, and rebellious.

Knowing the tendency of His people to wander, it makes perfect sense that God would give us copious examples of how to return to Him. Time and again— 12, to be exact[1]—the inspired Word tells us how God's people strayed and then found their way back to the Lord. Should we not glean wisdom and guidance from these accounts? Does it not seem beneficial for God's people today to read and study the inspired record of the power of return?

We can also read of the power of return in recent history. Such reading is fascinating and inspiring. Faith swells within us as we learn of how God moved in times past. What Christian has not thrilled to read of Wesley preaching in the fields to coal miners, Evan Roberts galvanizing Wales, or Jonathan Edwards sweeping congregants to the floor with powerful preaching? How our hearts burn when we read of the great Cane Ridge revival in Kentucky, where in 1869 some reports say as many as 25,000 people gathered from as far away as 200 miles. One eyewitness later described a vast crowd of people that seemed to be agitated as if by a storm. From the observer's vantage point he could see, "seven preachers all speaking at once, some on stumps, and some on wagons."[2] The Cane Ridge revival continued day and night for six days without intermission. (Spiritual awakenings in our own time encourage us even if they are in distant cities or countries.)

Any student of revival can tell you of his or her favorite historical account or regale you with stories of more contemporary times of refreshing. Sadly, few can tell of their favorite *biblical* revival. Yet, our truest guide for returning to the Lord is the holy Word of a God who still longs for our return. The great revivals of Scripture reveal the path and power of return.

Studying historical and even biblical revivals is certainly beneficial. Yet, wistfully regarding the record of heavenly fire falling is not sufficient. Enviously hearing of (and even watching) revival spring up in other locales is not satisfying. Those who hunger for a fresh outpouring must learn from the biblical record what is required for returning to the Lord and then must do these things with sincerity and repentant hearts.

There must be those who, like Joshua, are prepared and trained to rise up with the determination to lead the Church into the Promised Land of victorious living. Where are the Samuels who long to see the people return to God and conquer the fleshy inner enemy? We need more Davids who will not grow weary until the Ark of His presence rests again in the Lord's sanctuaries. Can we have some modern-day Solomons who obediently receive a vision to build? Asa's passion for seeking the Lord must be replicated among believers today. Jehoshaphat's zeal for the Lord and hatred for idolatry needs once again to cleanse our hearts and minds. The insistent and confrontational call heard in the courts of the Lord in Hezekiah's time must stir us to consecrate ourselves to God. Will we see more wise Jehoiadas determined to once again depose evil authority usurping the power of the true King? Josiah's vision of a people who "perform the words of the covenant written in the book" must become our present reality. Rebuilders like Zerubbabel must raise again a holy temple on the Cornerstone. Summon the godly Ezras whose hearts yearn to know, teach, and live the Word of God. May strong Nehemiahs pick up the sword in one hand and a trowel in the other to rebuild the wall of godly character. These will be the signs of a return to the Lord. Strive to emulate these great spiritual leaders of Israel and then stand ready; for the Lord has promised to return to the people who return to Him.

ENDNOTES

1. Twelve is a biblical number of some import (e.g., 12 tribes, 12 disciples, etc.).

2. Charles L. Thompson, *A History of American Revivals* (Chicago: M. W. Smith & Co., 1877, Reprinted by Christian Book Gallery, St. John, Indiana, 1990) 81.

AUTHOR'S MINISTRY PAGE

JOHN GOYETTE IS AVAILABLE FOR SPEAKING ENGAGEMENTS.

E-mail: greenmountainpastor@comcast.net

Office phone: 802-447-7224

Mailing address:

John Goyette
440 Main Street
Bennington, VT 05201

Please visit my Website at www.greenmtn.org.

The blog/Website for the book is

thepowerofreturn.com.

Additional copies of this book and other
book titles from DESTINY IMAGE are
available at your local bookstore.

Call toll-free: 1-800-722-6774.

Send a request for a catalog to:

Destiny Image₍ᵣ₎ Publishers, Inc.

P.O. Box 310
Shippensburg, PA 17257-0310

*"Speaking to the Purposes of God for This
Generation and for the Generations to Come."*

For a complete list of our titles,
visit us at www.destinyimage.com.